MW00674505

Study Guide to Accompany

Using Financial Accounting: An Introduction

Dennis Murray
University of Colorado at Denver

Bruce R. Neumann
University of Colorado at Denver

Pieter Elgers
University of Massachusetts—Amherst

Prepared by
Cecelia M. Fewox
Trident Technical College

West Publishing Company
Minneapolis/St. Paul New York Los Angeles San Francisco

WEST'S COMMITMENT TO THE ENVIRONMENT

In 1906, West Publishing Company began recycling materials left over from the production of books. This began a tradition of efficient and responsible use of resources. Today, 100% of our legal bound volumes are printed on acid-free, recycled paper consisting of 50% new fibers. West recycles nearly 27,700,000 pounds of scrap paper annually—the equivalent of 229,300 trees. Since the 1960s, West has devised ways to capture and recycle waste inks, solvents, oils, and vapors created in the printing process. We also recycle plastics of all kinds, wood, glass, corrugated cardboard, and batteries, and have eliminated the use of polystyrene book packaging. We at West are proud of the longevity and the scope of our commitment to the environment.

West pocket parts and advance sheets are printed on recyclable paper and can be collected and recycled with newspapers. Staples do not have to be removed. Bound volumes can be recycled after removing the cover.

Production, Prepress, Printing and Binding by West Publishing Company.

TEXT IS PRINTED ON 10% POST CONSUMER RECYCLED PAPER

04 03 02 01 00 99 98 97 8 7 6 5 4 3 2 1 0

ISBN 0–314–20976–X

CHAPTER 1

FINANCIAL ACCOUNTING AND ITS ENVIRONMENT

CHAPTER OVERVIEW

Chapter 1 introduces you to a variety of financial accounting topics. You will learn the difference between financial accounting (with its external user focus), management accounting (with its internal user focus), and tax accounting. You will learn about users of accounting information and how that information is delivered. How generally accepted accounting principles are determined and the role of auditing are discussed, as is the importance of ethics in accounting.

Review of Specific Chapter Objectives

1. Identify the objectives of accounting.

   ▲ The **primary objective of accounting** is to provide useful information to those who make business and economic decisions.

   ▲ A **secondary objective of accounting** is to help develop and enforce contracts.

2. Distinguish among the three major types of accounting.

   ▲ **Financial accounting** provides information to decision makers who are external to the business, e.g., present and future shareholders, present and future creditors, and government regulators.

   ▲ **Managerial accounting** provides information to decision makers who are internal to the business, i.e., managers of the company. This information is not published to people outside of the business.

▲ **Tax accounting** involves tax compliance (calculation of the company's tax liability after the transactions for a year have been completed) and tax planning (consideration of a transaction before it has taken place in order to determine tax consequences).

▲ **Accounting information systems** are the processes and procedures required to generate accounting information.

▲ **Nonbusiness organization accounting** deals with the accounting needs of organizations which do not attempt to earn a profit, such as hospitals, colleges, and churches.

3. List the three primary financial statements, and briefly summarize the information contained in each.

▲ The **financial accounting process** involves categorizing past transactions and events; measuring attributes of those transactions and events; and recording and summarizing the measurements. The initial valuation of a transaction, called the **historical cost**, is generally not changed in the future.

▲ The **end result of the accounting process** is the preparation of three major financial statements: the balance sheet, the income statement, and the statement of cash flows.

▲ The **balance sheet** shows a firm's assets, liabilities, and owners' equity at one point in time. **Assets** are valuable resources that a firm owns, while **liabilities** are obligations to convey something of value in the future. **Owners' equity** is a residual amount, calculated by subtracting liabilities from assets. (If assets are $300 and liabilities are $50, then owner's equity must equal $250.)

▲ The **income statement** summarizes a firm's revenues and expenses for a period of time. **Revenues** are inflows of assets from providing goods and services to customers, while **expenses** are the costs incurred to generate revenues. If revenues exceed expenses, then the result is net income; if expenses exceed revenues, then the result is a net loss. (If expenses are $500 and revenues are $400, then there is a net loss of $100.)

▲ The **statement of cash flows** summarizes a firm's inflows and outflows of cash over a period of time. The statement has **three sections**: operating activities, which deal with a company's operations; investing activities, which deal with a company's long-term asset transactions; and financing activities, which deal with a company's long-term debt activities and activities involving shareholders.

▲ Please note that the balance sheet reports its components as of one moment in time while the income statement and the statement of cash flows cover a period of time.

▲ **Notes to the financial statements**, which clarify and expand upon the material presented in the body of the statements, are an integral part of a set of financial statements. An example is a note which explains a company's inventory pricing policies or the methods used to depreciate fixed assets.

4. Identify financial statement users and the decisions they make.

▲ **Present and potential owners (investors)** assess and compare the prospects of alternative investments based on two variables: expected return (which refers to the increase in the investor's wealth that is expected over the investment's time horizon) and risk (which refers to the uncertainty surrounding estimates of expected return. Shareholders must decide whether to buy, hold, or sell shares in the firm.

▲ **Creditors** must decide whether to extend credit and on what terms.

▲ **Other users of financial statements** include financial analysts and advisors, customers, employees and labor unions, and regulatory authorities, such as the Securities and Exchange Commission and the Internal Revenue Service.

5. Explain how generally accepted accounting principles are determined.

▲ The most widely used set of accounting principles is called **generally accepted accounting principles (GAAP)**, currently set by the Financial Accounting Standards Board (FASB).

▲ The FASB uses a **due-process procedure** in setting standards in order to ensure that all interested parties are given an opportunity to have input into the standard-setting process.

▲ The **FASB's authority** derives from **two sources:** the acceptance of its rulings by the business community and the accounting profession and the delegation by the Securities and Exchange Commission of its legislative authority to determine GAAP for large, publicly held corporations.

6. Describe the role of auditing.

▲ While a firm's management is responsible for preparation of its financial statements, **independent certified public accountants (CPAs)** often perform audits in order to enhance the credibility of the statements. Please note that only a CPA may perform an audit.

- ▲ The **wording of the audit report is very specific** about what the audit does and does not do. Auditors follow **generally accepted auditing standards (GAAS)** in the conduct of the audit. GAAS are standards developed by the accounting profession to provide guidance in the performance of an audit.

- ▲ **An audit is not a guarantee of the correctness of the financial statements.** The audit report notes in the second paragraph that an audit provides reasonable, but not absolute, assurance that financial statements are free of material error. Auditors do not certify the financial statements.

- ▲ The **most desirable audit opinion** is the unqualified opinion.

7. List the economic consequences of the choice of accounting principles.

- ▲ With respect to standard-setting, the **FASB's primary objective** is to select accounting principles that provide useful information to financial statement readers. Accounting principles also have economic consequences to managers and their firms, and **managers consider these economic consequences when selecting accounting principles.**

- ▲ **Accounting principles have implementation costs and can affect the wealth of managers and firms via compensation plans, debt contracts, and political costs.**

- ▲ A **compensation plan** may tie managers' compensation to earnings, and therefore, the managers might choose principles which will enhance earnings.

- ▲ With respect to **debt contracts**, the use of accounting principles which increase reported net income can reduce the chances of contract violation.

- ▲ With respect to **political costs**, a firm might choose accounting principles which will minimize reported income in order to keep government regulation and taxation to a minimum.

8. Assess the importance of ethics in accounting.

- ▲ **Accountants have a significant responsibility to the public** because the public relies upon financial statements in order to make business decisions. It is imperative that accountants follow the highest ethical principles in order to keep that public trust in the profession.

- ▲ The American Institute of Certified Public Accountants

(AICPA) has a Code of Professional Conduct which emphasizes CPAs' obligation to serve the public interest.

CHAPTER SELF-TEST

Note: The notation (CO1) means that the question was drawn from chapter objective number one.

Matching

Please write the letters of the following terms in the spaces to the left of the definitions.

a. Assets
b. Expenses
c. Owners' Equity
d. Liabilities
e. Revenues

_____ 1. (CO3) Obligations of a business to convey something of value in the future.

_____ 2. (CO3) A residual amount on the balance sheet.

_____ 3. (CO3) Costs incurred to generate revenues.

_____ 4. (CO3) Inflows of assets from providing goods and services to customers.

_____ 5. (CO3) Valuable resources that a firm owns.

Completion

Please write in the word or words which will complete the sentence.

1. (CO1) The purpose of accounting is to provide useful ____________________ to those make business and economic ____________________.

2. (CO5) The most widely used set of accounting principles is referred to as ____________________ ____________________ ____________________ ____________________.

3. (CO3) The initial valuation at which an asset is recorded, and which generally is not subsequently changed, is called the ______________ ______________.

4. (CO2) ____________________ ____________________ provides information to decision makers who are external to the business.

5. (CO6) Rules developed by the accounting profession to provide guidance in the performance of an audit are called ______________ ______________ ______________ ______________.

6. (CO2) ______________ ______________ provides information to decision makers who are internal to the business.

Multiple Choice

Please circle the correct answer.

1. (CO3) Which of the following financial statements reports a company's revenues and expenses?
   a. Income statement.
   b. Statement of owners' equity.
   c. Balance sheet.
   d. Statement of cash flows.

2. (CO3) Which of the following financial statements provides information about a firm's operating, investing, and financing activities?
   a. Income statement.
   b. Statement of owners' equity.
   c. Balance sheet.
   d. Statement of cash flows.

3. (CO3) Which of the following financial statements provides information about a company for one moment in time?
   a. Income statement.
   b. Statement of owners' equity.
   c. Balance sheet.
   d. Statement of cash flows.

4. (CO4) The increase in the investor's wealth that is expected over the investment's time horizon is called the:
   a. investment selection.
   b. expected return.
   c. risk.
   d. None of the above is correct.

5. (CO5) Generally accepted accounting principles (GAAP) are currently set by the:
   a. Financial Accounting Standards Board.
   b. American Institute of Certified Public Accountants.
   c. Securities and Exchange Commission.
   d. Accounting Principles Board.

6. (CO5) The federal government regulatory agency which sets disclosure requirements for the corporations that it regulates is the:
   a. Financial Accounting Standards Board.
   b. American Institute of Certified Public Accountants.
   c. Securities and Exchange Commission.
   d. Accounting Principles Board.

7. (CO6) In order to enhance the credibility of its financial statements, a company will hire a CPA to __________ its financial statements.
   a. certify
   b. audit
   c. review
   d. guarantee

8. (CO3) If a company's revenues exceed its expenses, then it:
   a. has incurred a net loss.
   b. is at the break-even point.
   c. has earned net income.
   d. None of the above is correct.

9. (CO3) The numerical difference between a firm's assets and liabilities is called:
   a. net income.
   b. net loss.
   c. cash flow.
   d. owner's equity.

10. (CO8) Which of the following ethical frameworks judges the moral correctness of an act based solely upon its consequences?
    a. Utilitarianism.
    b. Unitarianism.
    c. Deontology.
    d. Phrenology.

Demonstration Problem

Wicket Company has an incentive plan for one of its managers. If the current year's net income is higher than last year's net income by $500,000, the manager will receive a $10,000 bonus. In December, the last month of the accounting period, the manager reviews the numbers and realizes that net income is higher by $475,000. He reviews company expenses and finds that warranty expense, which is based on estimates, could be lowered by $25,000. This will increase net income to the $500,000 target, and he will receive his bonus.

REQUIRED: Please discuss the propriety of lowering warranty expense. Include in your discussion ideas about economic consequences and managerial preferences for accounting principles. Who will be affected if the manager does lower the warranty expense estimate? (CO4, CO7, CO8)

SOLUTIONS TO SELF-TEST

Matching

1. d
2. c
3. b
4. e
5. a

Completion

1. information, decisions
2. generally accepted accounting principles
3. historical cost
4. Financial accounting
5. generally accepted auditing standards
6. Managerial accounting

Multiple Choice

1. a
2. d
3. c
4. b
5. a
6. c
7. b
8. c
9. d
10. a

Demonstration Problem

As noted in the text, accounting principles have implementation costs and can affect the wealth of managers and firms via compensation plans. In this case, because his bonus is tied to performance, the manager has a vested interest in choosing a principle which will benefit him. While warranty expense is based on an estimate, companies try to be as accurate as possible in their estimation procedures. The assumption is that the original estimate is correct. The estimate should be lowered only if new information indicates that the original estimate is incorrect. If the manager lowers the estimate only in order to achieve the target income and, thus, to receive his bonus, then he is acting unethically.

If the manager does lower the estimate in this unethical fashion, then the company will be affected since its financial statements will be inaccurate. It will also be taken by surprise when the actual warranty expense is higher than the lowered estimate indicates. Also affected will be any parties using and relying on the financial statements, such as potential and current owners, potential and current creditors, and regulatory authorities.

CHAPTER 2

BASIC CONCEPTS OF FINANCIAL ACCOUNTING

CHAPTER OVERVIEW

Chapter 2 expands on topics that you used in chapter 1. You will learn how to analyze transactions affecting companies and how to prepare simple balance sheets and income statements. You will learn about the accrual and the cash bases of accounting and will see how the balance sheets of sole proprietorships and of corporations differ.

Review of Specific Chapter Objectives

1. Define the terms assets, liabilities, and owners' equity.
2. Explain why the balance sheet must balance.

- ▲ Financial accounting is based upon the **accounting equation:** Assets = Liabilities + Owners' Equity. This is a mathematical equation which must balance. If assets total $300 and liabilities total $200, then owners' equity must be $100.

- ▲ **The balance sheet is an expanded expression of the accounting equation.**

- ▲ **Assets** are valuable resources that are owned by a firm. They represent probable future economic benefits and arise as the result of past transactions or events.

- ▲ **Liabilities** are present obligations of the firm. They are probable future sacrifices of economic benefits which arise as the result of past transactions or events.

- ▲ **Owners' equity** represents the owners' interest in the assets of the business. Owners may make a direct investment in the business or operate at a profit and leave the profit in the business. **Another name for owners' equity is** residual interest. **Yet another name** is net assets, indicating that owners' equity results when liabilities are subtracted from assets.

▲ **Both liabilities and owners' equity represent claims on the assets of a business.** The former are claims by people external to the business; the latter is a claim by the owners.

3. Describe revenues and expenses.

▲ **Revenues** are inflows of assets (or reductions in liabilities) in exchange for providing goods and services to customers. A retail store such as Wal-Mart earns revenues by selling goods to customers, while a CPA firm earns revenues by providing services such as tax return preparation or auditing.

▲ **A critically important point** is that cash need not be received in order for revenue to be recorded. Revenues are earned when a company does what it is supposed to do according to a contract. The company may receive in return for its goods or services cash or other assets, such as accounts receivable, which are promises by a customer or client to pay cash in the future.

▲ **A related concept** concerns cash received before a service is performed or goods are delivered. Consider the following example. A magazine company receives $24, which represents a year's subscription. The subscriber, of course, pays in advance. The magazine company may not record revenue because it has not earned revenue yet. To earn revenue, it must send the subscriber one magazine a month for twelve months. It owes magazines to the subscriber and thus has a liability (called Unearned Revenue), not revenue. As magazines are sent, revenues may be recorded. **Unearned revenues** are usually settled by the performance of a service, such as sending magazines, unlike other liabilities which are usually settled by the payment of cash.

▲ **Expenses** occur when resources are consumed in order to generate revenue. They are the cost of doing business. Examples include rent, salaries and wages, insurance, electricity, utilities, and the like.

▲ **A critically important point** similar to that for revenues holds true for expenses. A business need not pay out cash in order to have to record that an expense has occurred. If a repairman comes to the business to work on the air conditioning system, then the business has a repair expense even though that work may be charged to its account. The company will have a liability which it will settle later with the payment of cash.

▲ **Sales of inventory** contain both revenue and expense components. A **revenue transaction** exists because an asset has been obtained and goods have been provided to customers. An **expense transaction** exists because an asset has been consumed to generate the revenue. The resulting expense is called cost of goods sold.

▲ **Revenues increase owners' equity, while expenses decrease owners' equity.**

▲ **At the end of an accounting period,** before an income statement and a balance sheet can be prepared, **adjustments to certain accounts are almost always required.** A balance in an account may need to be adjusted because of the passage of time and the occurrence of events in that time period. In other cases, an amount may not have been recorded in an account at all, and the amount will have to be recorded before the financial statements are prepared so that all the information will be correct.

▲ **Interest** is a rental charge for the use of money. It is computed by multiplying the principal (or borrowed amount) by the interest rate and by the period of time involved. Since the interest rate is an annual rate, the time period must also be an annual period. If the time is given in months, then the time fraction will have 12 in the denominator. If the time is given in days, then the time fraction will have 360 (bobtail or banker's year) or 365 in the denominator. If a company has borrowed $12,000 at 10% for three months, and if one month has elapsed, then the interest which has accumulated, whether paid in cash or not, is computed as follows: $12,000 X .10 X 1/12, or $100. (The number 360 is used in the denominator because it eases computations. It is also used by some financial institutions because it results in more interest for them. Try multiplying $12,000 X 10% X 90/360. Now multiply $12,000 X 10% X 90/365. Which results in more interest?)

▲ If **rent is prepaid**, then as time elapses, the asset is used up, or consumed, and an expense is incurred. If a business prepays $6,000 for five months' worth of rent, and if two months have gone by, then the business has incurred $2,400 of expense ($1,200 per month for two months). The same is true for other items paid in advance, such as insurance.

▲ **Depreciation** shows that an asset such as equipment or a building is wearing out and being used up. Depreciation expense is computed by dividing the estimated useful life of the asset into the asset's historical cost (less any salvage value estimated by the business). If a machine cost $5,000 and has a salvage value of $500, with a useful life of five years, then the depreciation expense per year will be $900 ([$5,000 - $500] ÷ 5 years).

▲ If a company has **unearned revenue**, then it may have earned revenue as time has elapsed because it has provided the service to the customer. The liability "Unearned Revenue" will have to be decreased, and revenue will have to be recorded. Using the magazine example above, if three months' worth of magazines have been sent to the subscriber, then the company will reduce its liability and increase its revenues by $6 (3 months X $2/month).

▲ Remember that **four transactions affect owners' equity:**
Owner contributions increase owners' equity.
Owner withdrawals decrease owners' equity. (Withdrawals are for the personal use of the owner.)
Revenues increase owners' equity.
Expenses decrease owners' equity.

4. Use the basic accounting equation to analyze transactions.

▲ **Transaction analysis** is the central component of the financial accounting process.

▲ Remember that **every transaction must keep the accounting equation in balance.**

▲ **A transaction may do one of several things:** It may increase both the asset side and the liabilities and owners' equity side; it may decrease both the asset side and the liabilities and owners' equity side; it may cause both an increase and a decrease on the asset side; or it may cause both an increase and a decrease on the liabilities and owners' equity side. Regardless of what transaction occurs, the accounting equation must be in balance after the transaction is analyzed.

▲ The **entity assumption** dictates that business records must be kept separate and distinct from the personal records of the owners. If a person owns more than one business, then each business must have its own set of records.

▲ The **word "payable"** is usually used in a liability title. Examples are notes payable (written obligations), accounts payable (unwritten obligations that arise in the normal operations of a business), and wages payable.

▲ As you learned in chapter 1, **historical cost** is used for the recording of an asset. It is the exchange price on the date of the acquisition of the asset. Even though over time an asset's value may increase above the historical cost, that cost is still kept on the books because the number is considered to be reliable.

5. Prepare simple balance sheets and income statements.

▲ The **end result of the accounting process** is the preparation of financial statements.

▲ Please remember from chapter 1 that the **balance sheet** shows a firm's assets, liabilities, and owner's equity at one point in time. The date on the balance sheet will be a single date, such as December 31 or June 30.

▲ The **income statement** summarizes a firm's revenues and expenses for a period of time. The date on the income statement will be a phrase such as, "For the month ended July 31," or "For the year ended December 31." Remember that if revenues exceed expenses, then the result is net income; if expenses exceed revenues, then the result is a net loss. Remember that **only revenues and expenses appear on the income statement.** Students sometimes think that cash is a good thing and should appear on the income statement, but remember that cash is an asset and so will appear on the balance sheet.

▲ The **statement of owners' equity** summarizes the changes that took place in owners' equity during the period under review. It will have the same date as does the income statement: It shows results over a period of time, not just at one point in time. The statement starts with the beginning balance of owners' equity and adds in any owner investment and net income. If there are withdrawals, then they are subtracted, as is a net loss. Remember that a business will have either a net income or a net loss, not both.

6. Describe the relationship between the balance sheet and the income statement.

▲ **Changes in net income, owner contributions, and owner withdrawals, all of which affect owners' equity, explain changes in net assets.**

7. Distinguish between the accrual basis and the cash basis of accounting.

▲ The **accrual basis of accounting** records revenues when goods have been delivered or services have been performed, regardless of when cash is received. This basis also records expenses when resources are consumed, regardless of when payment is made.

▲ The **cash basis of accounting** records revenue when cash is received. This basis also records expenses when cash is paid.

▲ The **accrual basis** is preferable for providing the most useful information to financial statement users. **GAAP requires use of the accrual basis.**

▲ **Use of the accrual basis keeps in place the matching principle**, which states that all resources consumed in generating revenue should be shown on the same income statement (that is, during the same time period) as that revenue.

8. Explain the differences between the balance sheets of sole proprietorships and those of corporations.

▲ **Sole proprietorships** are businesses that are owned by one individual and usually operated by that individual. Their **primary advantage** is ease of formation; their **major disadvantage** is unlimited liability. Because of the **entity assumption**, records of the business and its owner must be kept separate.

▲ **Partnerships** consist of two or more persons in business to make a profit. They are very similar to sole proprietorships.

▲ **Corporations**, unlike proprietorships or partnerships, are separate legal entities. They are more difficult to form, and they must pay income taxes. If shareholders receive dividends, then those dividends are taxable, leading to double taxation of income. A **major advantage** of a corporation is the limited liability of its shareholders: Only a shareholder's investment in the corporation is at risk.

▲ **Balance sheet differences** lie mainly in the equity section. A sole proprietorship has one capital account (while in a partnership, each partner has his or her own capital account). **Shareholders' equity** of a corporation, however, consists of two components: invested capital, which results from direct contributions by the shareholders; and retained earnings, which reflects the increases and decreases in the shareholders' interest in the company that arose from operations since the company's inception.

CHAPTER SELF-TEST

Note: The notation (CO1) means that the question was drawn from chapter objective number one.

Matching

Please write the letters of the following terms in the spaces to the left of the definitions.

a. Accounts payable
b. Accounts receivable
c. Cost of goods sold
d. Net assets
e. Prepaid rent
f. Unearned revenue

_____ 1. (CO1) Represents a right to receive cash in the future.

_____ 2. (CO1) Another name for owners' equity.

_____ 3. (CO3) A liability; represents money received in advance obligating a firm to provide goods or services in the future.

_____ 4. (CO1) Represents an obligation to pay cash in the future.

_____ 5. (CO3) An asset; represents money paid in advance for the future delivery of goods or providing of services.

_____ 6. (CO3) An expense which represents that the asset inventory has been consumed to generate revenue for a business.

Completion

Please write in the word or words which will complete the sentence.

1. (CO1) The balance sheet is the expanded expression of the ____________________ ____________________ ______________.

2. (CO7) The ____________________ basis of accounting records revenues when earned and expenses when incurred, regardless of when cash is received.

3. (CO2) The ____________________ assumption dictates that records for a business must be kept separate from the personal records of the owner or owners.

4. (CO7) The ________________________ principle states that all resources consumed in generating revenue should be shown during the same accounting period as is the revenue.

5. (CO8) For a corporation, the shareholders' equity section of the balance sheet consists of ________________________ ________________________ and ________________________.

6. (CO7) The ________________________ basis of accounting records revenues when cash is received and expenses when cash is paid.

Multiple Choice

Please circle the correct answer.

1. (CO3) What is the effect on the accounting equation when a business performs services on account for a client?
   a. Assets increase; owners' equity decreases.
   b. Assets increase; liabilities increase.
   c. Assets increase; owners' equity increases.
   d. Assets decrease; owners' equity decreases.

2. (CO3) What is the effect on the accounting equation when a business pays a liability that it had previously recorded?
   a. Assets decrease; liabilities decrease.
   b. Assets decrease; owners' equity decreases.
   c. Assets increase; liabilities increase.
   d. Liabilities decrease; owners' equity decreases.

3. (CO4) A company purchases a delivery van for $20,000. It expects to use it for five years, after which it expects to sell it for $4,000. What is the monthly depreciation on the van?
   a. $5,000.
   b. $3,200.
   c. $ 333.
   d. $ 267.

4. (CO7) Wahoo Company performed services for a customer in January. The customer promised to pay in February, but Wahoo didn't receive a check until March. In what month should Wahoo record the revenue if it uses the accrual basis of accounting?
   a. January.
   b. February.
   c. March.
   d. December (year-end for Wahoo).

5. (CO8) Which of the following forms of business organization is a separate legal entity?
   a. Partnership.
   b. Corporation.
   c. Sole proprietorship.
   d. None of the above is a separate legal entity.

6. (CO2) Another name for owners' equity is:
   a. net liabilities.
   b. net assets.
   c. net worth.
   d. Both b and c are correct.

7. (CO3) What effect does an owner withdrawal have on owners' equity?
   a. Since a withdrawal is an expense, it decreases owners' equity.
   b. A withdrawal increases owners' equity.
   c. A withdrawal decreases owners' equity.
   d. A withdrawal has no effect on owners' equity.

8. (CO3) What effect do revenues and expenses have on owners' equity?
   a. Revenues--increase; expenses--increase.
   b. Revenues--decrease; expenses--decrease.
   c. Revenues--increase; expenses--decrease.
   d. Revenues--decrease; expenses--increase.

9. (CO3) Owners' equity at the beginning of January was $10,000. During January there was an owner contribution of $1,000; the owner also withdrew $200. Net income for January was $3,500. What was owners' equity at the end of January?
   a. $14,300.
   b. $13,500.
   c. $12,700.
   d. It cannot be determined from the information given.

10. (CO2) Assets on December 31 were $25,000. Owners' equity on December 1 was $13,000, and net income for December was $5,000. What is the dollar amount of <u>liabilities</u> on <u>December 31</u>?
   a. $ 7,000.
   b. $12,000.
   c. $20,000.
   d. It cannot be determined from the information given.

Demonstration Problem

The following are the account balances for Little Company for November 30, 1998:

Cash	$ 3,000
Accounts Receivable	4,000
Inventory	12,000
Supplies	500
Accounts Payable	2,500
Salaries Payable	1,000
Notes Payable	5,000

The Little, Capital account had a balance of $5,000 on November 1. Revenues for November totaled $20,000, expenses totaled $13,000, and Little withdrew $1,000 for his personal use during the month.

REQUIRED: Please prepare the income statement and the statement of owner's equity (Little is a sole proprietor) for the month of November and the balance sheet as of November 30. (CO5)

SOLUTIONS TO SELF-TEST

Matching

1. b
2. d
3. f
4. a
5. e
6. c

Completion

1. basic accounting equation
2. accrual
3. entity
4. matching
5. invested capital, retained earnings
6. cash

Multiple Choice

1. c
2. a
3. d
4. a
5. b
6. d
7. c
8. c
9. a
10. a

Demonstration Problem

Little Company
Income Statement
For the Month Ended November 30, 1998

Revenues	$20,000
Expenses	13,000
Net Income	$ 7,000

Little Company
Statement of Owner's Equity
For the Month Ended November 30, 1998

Balance, November 1	$ 5,000
Net Income	7,000
Withdrawal	(1,000)
Balance, November 30	$11,000

Little Company
Balance Sheet
November 30, 1998

Assets	
Cash	$ 3,000
Accounts Receivable	4,000
Inventory	12,000
Supplies	500
Total Assets	$19,500
Liabilities and Owner's Equity	
Liabilities	
Accounts Payable	$ 2,500
Salaries Payable	1,000
Notes Payable	5,000
Total Liabilities	$ 8,500
Owner's Equity	
Little, Capital	11,000
Total Liabilities and Owner's Equity	$19,500

Please note that net income from the income statement carries forward to the statement of owner's equity and that the ending balance on the statement of owner's equity carries forward to the balance sheet.

CHAPTER 3

THE BALANCE SHEET

CHAPTER OVERVIEW

Chapter 3 expands your knowledge of the balance sheet. It reviews the accounting equation and then shows how the balance sheet is the expanded expression of the equation. It provides an in-depth discussion of the types of assets and liabilities commonly on the balance sheet and shows how relationships between various items help analysts to gauge the strength or weakness of a business.

Review of Specific Chapter Objectives

1. Identify the basic elements of the balance sheet.

- ▲ Remember that the **basic accounting equation** states that assets equal the sum of liabilities and owners' equity.

- ▲ The **balance sheet,** also called the Statement of Financial Position, is the expanded expression of the accounting equation. Another way to state the equation is this: Uses of Resources = Sources of Resources. Liabilities and owners' equity are the sources from which the firm has obtained its funds, and the listing of assets shows the way that the firm's managers have put those funds to work.

- ▲ The balance sheet is the **cumulative result of the firm's past activities.**

- ▲ **Assets** are probable future economic benefits obtained or controlled by a particular entity as a result of past transactions or events.

- ▲ **Liabilities** are probable future sacrifices of economic benefits arising from present obligations of a particular entity to transfer assets or provide services to other entities in the future as a result of past transactions or events.

▲ **Owners' equity** is the residual interest in the assets of an entity after deducting liabilities.

2. Recognize the types of assets, liabilities, and owners' equity that are found on the balance sheets of most business firms.
3. Comprehend the ordering and classification of items on the balance sheet.

▲ Regardless of the type of asset, **all assets have a common characteristic in representing probable future economic benefits to the firm.**

▲ Assets are divided into **two overall categories: current and noncurrent.** Current assets are those assets which will typically become cash or be consumed in one year or one operating cycle, whichever is greater. Noncurrent assets are assets used in the conduct of the business and for which the replacement cycle is longer than one year.

▲ **Current assets are listed in order of their maturity or collectibility (or liquidity,** which reflects the ability of the firm to generate sufficient cash to meet its operating cash needs and to pay its obligations as they become due). Because of the liquidity focus, **current assets are generally valued at the lower of their acquisition costs or present resale values.**

▲ **Cash and cash equivalents** include currency, bank deposits, and various marketable securities that can be turned into cash on short notice merely by contacting a bank or broker. (Cash equivalents are only securities purchased within ninety days of their maturity dates.) Cash is often considered to be any item which a bank will accept at face value for deposit. If you receive a pig in a bartering transaction, then the pig is not considered cash. Try depositing the pig into your account at the bank!

▲ **Accounts receivable** represent credit sales that have not yet been collected. A fast turnover period for accounts receivable is desirable: The longer a debt remains unpaid, the higher the chance that it will not ever be paid. Accounts receivable are listed on the balance sheet at their net realizable value, which is the amount management thinks it will actually be able to collect.

▲ **Inventory** represents items that have been purchased or manufactured for resale to customers. Some students feel that inventory should be reported as a noncurrent asset, but ask yourself this question: Does a business, which earns money by selling goods, really want its inventory to remain unsold for over one year? Remember that stores have sales in order to move out slowly moving inventory. Just as is true for accounts receivable, a fast turnover period for inventory is very desirable. At times it is necessary for reporting purposes to reduce the historical cost of the inventory to a lower value.

▲ The **operating cycle of a business** is the time which elapses from the purchase of inventory, to the exchange of inventory for accounts receivable, to the collection of that receivable. It is sometimes called the cash-to-cash cycle because it is the time which elapses from the time a company spends money to purchase inventory to the time it receives cash for that inventory. Some businesses have a very short operating cycle, a week or two, while others have operating cycles which take years (for example, companies in the forest products industry or the distilled spirits industry).

▲ **Noncurrent assets**, as noted above, are assets used in the conduct of the business and for which the replacement cycle is longer than one year. Whereas the focus for current assets is their liquidity, the **focus for noncurrent assets is on the operating capacity of the firm.**

▲ **Property, plant, and equipment** comprises the most common type of noncurrent assets. **Property** usually represents the land upon which the firm's offices, factories, and other facilities are located. It is valued on the balance sheet at its historical acquisition cost which, because of the age of the land, is often the most out of date in terms of current market values.

▲ **Buildings or plant** may include buildings, warehouses, hospitals, and myriad other assets. **Equipment** includes office furniture, tools, computers, and the like. **Buildings and equipment are the primary productive assets of any organization.**

▲ Because **property, plant, and equipment assets wear out over time**, they must be reported on the balance sheet at their net book value: their cost less Accumulated Depreciation. Accumulated Depreciation is the total amount of depreciation expense that has been recognized to date. If an asset's cost is $10,000 and the Accumulated Depreciation account shows a balance of $2,000, then the net book value is $8,000. **Depreciation** is a rational and systematic allocation of an asset's cost to expense over the asset's life. It has nothing to do with writing assets up or down to market value or attempting to accumulate cash for the purpose of replacing the asset.

▲ Another noncurrent asset class is the group called **intangible**

assets. These lack physical substance and yet are important resources in the regular operations of a business. **Patents**, which protect invention, and **copyrights**, which protect artistic works, are examples of intangible assets. **Goodwill** denotes the economic value of an acquired firm in excess of the value of its identifiable net assets (assets minus liabilities). Pooky Company has assets of $500,000 and liabilities of $300,000. Therefore, its net assets are $200,000. If Cassie Company pays $250,000 to buy Pooky Company, then there is goodwill of $50,000 ($250,000 - $200,000). Goodwill may only be recorded when one business buys another business. Internally generated goodwill may not be recorded in the accounting records. Very often the most important asset of a business is its personnel, or human resources, but human resources does not appear on the balance sheet as an asset class. There are also other assets which do not appear on the balance sheet, such as customers and suppliers.

- ▲ **Liabilities** include any probable obligation that the firm has incurred as a consequence of its past activities. While some liabilities involve a specific dollar amount on a specific date, others involve estimates.

- ▲ Just as was true for assets, there are **two overall categories of liabilities: current and noncurrent**. Current liabilities are short-term obligations that are expected to utilize cash or other current assets within a year or an operating cycle, whichever is longer. Noncurrent liabilities represent obligations that generally require payment over periods longer than a year.

- ▲ **Current liabilities include accounts payable, notes payable, warranty obligations and accrued expenses. Accounts payable** represent debts that the firm incurs in purchasing inventories and supplies for manufacturing or resale purposes. They also include anything that a firm purchases on credit.

- ▲ **Notes payable** are more formal current liabilities than the accounts payable. Notes are usually written documents which involve payment of interest.

- ▲ **Warranty obligations** represent the firm's estimated future costs to fulfill its obligations for repair or refund guarantees. Warranties are reported on **estimates** because a company cannot know for sure how many items will be returned for warranty work.

- ▲ **Accrued expenses** represent liabilities for services already consumed but not yet paid for or included elsewhere in liabilities.

- **Taxes payable** represent unpaid taxes owed to a governmental unit and will be paid within one year.

- **Noncurrent liabilities**, as noted above, represent obligations that generally require payment over periods longer than a year. They are contracts to repay debt at specified future dates and often place some restrictions on the activities of the firm until the debt is fully repaid.

- **Bonds payable** are a major source of funds for larger companies. When it issues bonds, a company obligates itself to make periodic interest payments and to pay back the entire principal at the maturity date. A company usually issues bonds when the amount it is borrowing is too large to borrow from one source.

- A **mortgage payable** also involves payment of principal and interest, but it also represents a pledge of certain assets that will revert to the lender if the debt is not paid.

- Be aware that **a company sometimes has liabilities which do not appear on face of the balance sheet: They may only be disclosed in the notes to the financial statements.** An example is a lawsuit.

- As you learned in chapter 2, **owners' equity** represents the owners' claims on the assets of the business. Arithmetically, it is the difference between assets and liabilities. A **corporation's shareholders' equity** consists of two items: paid-in capital, which represents the direct investments by the owners of the firm, and retained earnings, which represent the earnings of the firm that have been reinvested in the business. An important point to remember is that retained earnings do not represent cash available for the payment of dividends. The Retained Earnings account is the cumulative story of all the income the firm has earned, all the losses it has incurred, and all the dividends it has paid out to shareholders.

4. Appreciate why balance sheets differ for firms in different industries.

   - **To a large extent, the composition of assets depends upon the industry in which a firm operates.** A company in the steel and automobile industries will own many property, plant and equipment assets while a company in the retail industry will show a high dollar amount of inventory but may show only one building on one piece of land.

5. Use balance sheet relationships to obtain information useful to investors and lenders.

▲ **Numbers on the balance sheet can be compared in order to gauge the financial strength or weakness of a company.** Please remember that such comparisons, in the form of ratios, are useful only when they are compared with something else, such as that company's ratio in former years or industry average ratios. Ratios are based on past data, which may be problematic, and they are also only as good as the data that comprise them.

▲ **Vertical analysis, or vertical percentage analysis,** involves stating a firm's individual assets in percentage terms of total assets. Individual liabilities and owners' equity items are stated in percentage terms of total liabilities and owners' equity.

▲ **Liquidity ratios** represent the ability of a company to convert its assets to cash. The current ratio is computed by dividing total current assets by total current liabilities. What a "good" current ratio is for a company depends on the industry in which the company operates. The quick ratio, or acid-test ratio, is computed by dividing "quick" assets by current liabilities. "Quick" assets are cash, cash equivalents, and net receivables: Inventory and prepaid expenses are excluded. Because the last two items mentioned are excluded, the quick ratio always will be less than the current ratio. Again, what a "good" quick ratio is depends on the industry in which a company operates.

▲ **Asset management ratios** focus on the composition of the firm's assets as well as changes in the composition of assets over time.

▲ **Debt management ratios** include the debt-to-assets ratio, which is computed by dividing total debt by total assets. This ratio indicates the firm's changing reliance on borrowed resources. The lower the ratio, the lower the firm's risk because the organization will usually be better able to meet its obligations for interest and debt payments.

6. Be alert to the limitations as well as the usefulness of balance sheet information.

▲ **Ratio calculations are only the first step in analyzing a firm's condition.**

▲ **Individual financial statements, such as the balance sheet, are seldom analyzed separately from other statements.**

▲ **Information useful for analyzing and clarifying financial statements is contained in other parts of a company's financial reports,** such as the notes to the financial statements.

- ▲ **Different accounting methods used by businesses will have different effects on the balance sheet numbers** and therefore, on the ratios derived by using balance sheet accounts.

CHAPTER SELF-TEST

Note: The notation (CO1) means that the question was drawn from chapter objective number one.

Matching

Please write the letters of the following terms in the spaces to the left of the definitions.

a. Amortization
b. Current ratio
c. Depreciation
d. Goodwill
e. Liquidity
f. Net realizable value
g. Operating capacity
h. Quick ratio

_____ 1. (CO2,3) Focus for reporting noncurrent assets of a business.

_____ 2. (CO5) Current assets divided by current liabilities.

_____ 3. (CO2,3) The ability of a firm to generate sufficient cash to meet its operating cash needs and to pay its obligations as they become due.

_____ 4. (CO3) Systematic and rational allocation of the cost of an intangible asset to expense.

_____ 5. (CO2,3) Must be generated externally in order to be recorded in the accounting records.

_____ 6. (CO5) The sum of cash and cash equivalents and net receivables divided by current liabilities.

_____ 7. (CO2,3) Systematic and rational allocation of the cost of property, plant, and equipment assets to expense.

_____ 8. (CO2,3) Dollar amount of accounts receivable realistically expected to be collectible.

Completion

Please write in the word or words which will complete the sentence.

1. (CO2,3) The time which elapses from the time a company spends cash to purchase inventory to the time that it collects cash for the sale of the inventory is called the ____________ ____________.

2. (CO2,3) A liability which requires payment over a period longer than a year is called a ____________ liability.

3. (CO2,3) Goodwill which is ____________ generated may not be recorded in the accounting records.

4. (CO5) ____________ ratios measure the ability of a company to convert its assets to cash.

5. (CO5) ____________ ____________ ratios focus on the composition of a firm's assets as well as changes in the composition of assets over time.

6. (CO2,3) Only securities purchased within ____________ days of their maturity dates may be classified as cash equivalents.

7. (CO2,3) ____________ assets include cash and other assets that will typically become cash or be consumed in one year or one operating cycle, whichever is greater.

8. (CO2,3) ____________ represents items that have been purchased or manufactured for resale to customers.

Multiple Choice

Please circle the correct answer.

1. (CO2,3) Which of the following will appear first in a list of current assets?
   a. Inventory.
   b. Accounts receivable.
   c. Prepaid expenses.
   d. Land.

2. (CO2,3) If the cost of a building is $425,000 and Accumulated Depreciation totals $100,000, then the net book value of the building is:
   a. $525,000.
   b. $425,000.
   c. $325,000.
   d. It cannot be determined from the information given.

3. (CO2,3) Accumulated depreciation:
   a. represents the total amount of depreciation expense that has been recognized up to a certain date.
   b. represents a company's attempt to adjust carrying values to current resale value.
   c. represents cash that a company has set aside for replacing a property, plant, and equipment asset.
   d. is none of the above.

4. (CO2,3) Short-term obligations expected to utilize cash or other current assets within the longer of a year or an operating cycle are called:
   a. current assets.
   b. noncurrent assets.
   c. noncurrent liabilities.
   d. current liabilities.

5. (CO2,3) A company's estimated future costs to fulfill its obligations for repair or refund guarantees are called:
   a. mortgages payable.
   b. warranty obligations.
   c. accounts payable.
   d. bonds payable.

6. (CO5) Consider the following data:

Cash and cash equivalents	$200,000
Inventory	300,000
Accounts payable	275,000
Accounts receivable	150,000
Bonds payable	200,000

   The current ratio for the company is:
   a. 2.36.
   b. 1.37.
   c. 1.27.
   d. .73.

7. (CO5) Consider the following data:

Cash and cash equivalents	$200,000
Inventory	300,000
Accounts payable	275,000
Accounts receivable	150,000
Bonds payable	200,000

The quick ratio for the company is:
a. 2.36.
b. 1.37.
c. 1.27.
d. .73.

8. (CO5) Analysis of a company which begins with the preparation of a common-size balance sheet, which shows the percentage component of each major section to the grand totals on each side of the balance sheet, is called:
a. liquidity analysis.
b. asset management analysis.
c. horizontal analysis.
d. vertical analysis.

9. (CO2,3) An asset which lacks physical substance is called:
a. a property, plant and equipment asset.
b. an intangible asset.
c. a current asset.
d. None of the above is correct.

10. (CO2,3) An example of an asset which is not listed on a company's balance sheet is:
a. externally generated goodwill.
b. a patent.
c. employees.
d. prepaid expenses.

Demonstration Problem

The following are data from the records of Cassandra Company as of June 30, 1998:

Cash and cash equivalents	$125,000
Prepaid expenses	5,000
Inventory	200,000
Accounts receivable	175,000
Accounts payable	100,000
Salaries payable	24,000
Notes payable	75,000
Land	300,000
Building	500,000
Accumulated depreciation	50,000
Mortgage payable	600,000
Bonds payable	400,000
Retained earnings	475,000
Invested capital	250,000

REQUIRED:

1. Please prepare in good form a classified balance sheet (CO2, CO3).
2. Please compute the current and quick ratios for the company (CO5).

1.

2.

SOLUTIONS TO SELF-TEST

Matching

1. g
2. b
3. e
4. a
5. d
6. h
7. c
8. f

Completion

1. operating cycle
2. noncurrent
3. internally
4. Liquidity
5. Asset management
6. 90
7. Current
8. Inventory

Multiple Choice

1. b
2. c
3. a
4. d
5. b
6. a
7. c
8. d
9. b
10. c

Demonstration Problem

1.

Cassandra Company
Balance Sheet
December 31, 1998

Assets			
Current Assets			
Cash and Cash Equivalents		$225,000	
Accounts Receivable		375,000	
Inventory		200,000	
Prepaid Expenses		55,000	
Total Current Assets			$ 855,000
Property, Plant and Equipment			
Land		619,000	
Building	$500,000		
Less: Acc. Depr.	50,000		
Net Book Value		450,000	
Total Property, Plant and Equipment			1,069,000
Total Assets			$1,924,000
Liabilities and Owners' Equity			
Current Liabilities			
Accounts Payable		$100,000	
Salaries Payable		24,000	
Notes Payable		375,000	
Total Current Liabilities			$ 499,000
Noncurrent Liabilities			
Mortgage Payable		300,000	
Bonds Payable		400,000	
Total Noncurrent Liabilities			700,000
Total Liabilities			1,199,000
Owners' Equity			
Retained Earnings		475,000	
Invested Capital		250,000	
Total Owners' Equity			725,000
Total Liabilities and Owners' Equity			$1,924,000

2. Current Ratio:

$$\frac{\$855{,}000}{\$499{,}000} = 1.7 \text{ (rounded)}$$

Quick Ratio:

$$\frac{\$225{,}000 + \$375{,}000}{\$499{,}000} = 1.2 \text{ (rounded)}$$

CHAPTER 4

THE INCOME STATEMENT

CHAPTER OVERVIEW

Chapter 4 expands your knowledge of the income statement. It shows the basic elements of the statement, two possible formats, and unusual items which are shown separately at the bottom of the statement. It discusses several generally accepted accounting principles which affect the income statement and shows how to compute several ratios using statement information.

Review of Specific Chapter Objectives

Introduction

▲ **Four major types of items appear on income statements:** **revenues, expenses, gains, and losses**.

▲ **Revenues** are inflows of assets (or reductions in liabilities) from providing goods and services to customers. It is important to note that revenues arise from the firm's **ongoing, central operations.**

▲ **Expenses** arise from consuming resources in order to generate revenue. As is true for revenues, expenses arise from the firm's **ongoing, central operations.**

▲ **Gains** increase assets or decrease liabilities. A gain differs from a revenue, however, in that gains arise from **peripheral transactions** of the business. A paper company earns revenues by selling paper. If it sells extra equipment from the employee lounge for more than the equipment's carrying value, then it will have a gain, not revenue.

▲ **Losses** decrease assets or increase liabilities. A loss differs from an expense, however, in that losses arise from **peripheral transactions** of the business. Returning to the above example, if the paper company sells that extra equipment for less than its carrying value, then it will have a loss, not an expense.

▲ The **materiality principle** states that separate disclosure on a financial statement is not required if an item is so small that knowledge of it would not affect the decision of a reasonable financial statement reader.

▲ **Net sales** is the difference between gross sales and certain items, such as sales returns. **Gross margin** is the difference between net sales and cost of goods sold.

▲ **Selling expenses** include any expenses necessary for the sale of goods, such as advertising and commissions. **Administrative expenses** include expenses related to the administration of the business, such as management salaries and legal and accounting fees.

▲ **Operating income** is the difference between gross margin and selling and administrative expenses. When interest and income tax expense are deducted from operating income, the result is **net income.**

Net sales
- Cost of goods sold

Gross margin
- Selling and administrative expenses

Operating income
- Interest expense
- Income tax expense

Net income

▲ Please remember the following important difference: **Revenue** refers to the total inflow of assets or reduction in liabilities, while **profit** is the net increase in a firm's recorded wealth after deducting expenses.

▲ Income statements may be presented in **several different formats**. The outline shown above is the multiple-step income statement, which shows various relationships. Another format is the single-step format, which adds up all revenues and all expenses and does a single step, a subtraction, with the totals.

▲ **A major purpose of the income statement** is to show a firm's profitability. Investors, lenders, and company management all use income statement information for their assorted purposes.

1. Explain when to recognize revenues.

▲ One of the generally accepted accounting principles is the **revenue recognition principle**, which states that revenue should be recognized in the accounting records when the earnings process is substantially complete and the amount to be collected is reasonably determinable. In most cases, revenue is recognized at the point of sale. Remember that revenue is earned, and thus recorded, whether or not cash is received: Payment for a good or service may be in the form of cash or an account receivable.

▲ There are **several exceptions to the revenue recognition principle.** If a seller is highly uncertain about the collectibility of receivables, then he should not recognize revenue until he receives cash. With respect to long-term construction contracts, a contractor may use the percentage-of-completion method to record revenues and profits periodically (he must be able to estimate the percentage of completeness of a contract in order to be able to use this method). Another exception is certain service contracts.

▲ **A company ought to disclose its revenue recognition policies** in the notes to the financial statements.

2. Explain when to recognize expenses.

▲ The **matching principle drives expense recognition.** It states that costs incurred to generate revenue appearing on the income statement in a given period should appear on the income statement in that same period.

▲ The **matching principle is implemented in one of three ways.** First is association of cause and effect, which implies that there is a clear and direct relationship between an expense and a revenue. Second is systematic and rational allocation, which is used when a cost cannot be directly linked to specific revenue transactions. Instead, the cost is simply allocated over time. Third is immediate recognition, used when costs have no discernable future benefit and thus are expensed immediately.

3. Interpret the components of the income statement.

▲ **Income statements summarize past transactions and events,** but many financial statement **users are** concerned **about** the **future, about earnings sustainability.** GAAP requires that income statements report certain items (discontinued operations and extraordinary items) separately from ongoing operations.

- ▲ **Discontinued operations** occur when a firm ceases, or plans to cease, operating, a major segment of its business. There are **two line items:** the results of operating the segment and the loss realized on the disposal. These **items are shown net of income tax.** Since there is presumably a loss on discontinued operations, the tax effect is a tax benefit because losses lower the taxes a firm must pay. To make predictions about future earnings, most analysts will add back the losses to reported net earnings to obtain adjusted net earnings because the discontinued operations results will not recur in the future.

- ▲ **Extraordinary items** are events and transactions that are unusual in nature and infrequent in occurrence. Evaluating both of those characteristics requires great judgment on the part of the accountant who decides whether or not an item is extraordinary. These items, such as natural disasters and a foreign government's expropriation of a firm's assets, are also **shown net of income tax.** An extraordinary item may be either a gain or a loss.

- ▲ **Earnings per share must be disclosed on the face of the income statement.** It is computed by dividing net income by the average number of shares of stock outstanding. If net income is $100,000, and there are 200,000 shares of stock outstanding, then earnings per share is $ .50 ($100,000 ÷ 200,000).

4. Analyze income statement information using various ratios.

- ▲ **Vertical analysis** examines relationships within a given year. This is accomplished by dividing each line of the income statement by the first item, which is net sales. This yields common-size income statements in percentage terms. The top line will always be 100% because net sales divided by itself yields 100%. A lower cost of goods sold percentage and a higher gross profit percentage are desirable. The operating income percentage is a measure of **management's success** in operating the firm, while the net income percentage is a measure of the firm's overall profitability.

- ▲ **Trend analysis** involves comparing financial statement numbers over a period of time. One way to accomplish this is to compare the common-size income statement items over a period of time. Another form of trend analysis is horizontal analysis, which uses the figures from a prior year's income statement as the base year for calculating percentage increases over a period of time. Assume that net income for 1996 is $100,000 and for 1997 is $110,000. Net income has thus increased by $10,000. If the $10,000 increase is divided by the 1996 base year net income number of $100,000, then the accountant can see that net income has increased by 10% from one year to the next.

- ▲ The **return on shareholders' equity (ROE) ratio** is computed by dividing net income by average shareholders' equity. This ratio relates earnings to the assets invested by its shareholders and is very important to investors. To compute average shareholders' equity, the accountant adds the beginning-of-the-year and the end-of-the-year shareholders' equity balances and then divides the total by 2.

- ▲ The **return on assets (ROA) ratio** relates a firm's earnings to all assets the firm has available to generate those earnings. It is computed by dividing average total assets into the sum of net income and interest expense (net of income tax).

- ▲ The **times interest earned ratio** shows how many times interest expense is covered by resources generated from operations and is very important to creditors of a business. It is computed by dividing earnings before interest and taxes by interest expense. Certainly a creditor would prefer a high number instead of a low number for this ratio.

- ▲ Please be aware that there are **limitations of accounting income**. For some assets, an increase in value is recognized only at the disposal of the asset. Financial statements, too, often do not reflect accomplishments of a firm, as in the case of an executory contract. The **conservatism principle**, one of the generally accepted accounting principles, also may limit the extent to which accounting income reflects changes in wealth. This principle states that when given a choice between or among acceptable alternatives for treatment for a transaction, the accountant should choose the alternative which least overstates assets and income.

5. Describe the effects that reported earnings have on managers' wealth and consequently, on their accounting policy decisions.

- ▲ **Bonuses** can motivate a company's managers to make accounting-related decisions that do not affect the underlying profitability of the company but that do affect reported accounting income. Because managers' self-interests influence their accounting policy judgments, financial statements may not be an unbiased reflection of the underlying economic activities of a firm.

CHAPTER SELF-TEST

Note: The notation (CO1) means that the question was drawn from chapter objective number one.

Matching

Please write the letters of the following terms in the spaces to the left of the definitions.

a. Cost of goods sold
b. Expenses
c. Gains
d. Gross margin
e. Losses
f. Net sales
g. Operating income
h. Revenues

_____ 1. (Intro) Inflows of assets, or reduction in liabilities, from providing goods and services to customers.

_____ 2. (Intro) Net sales less cost of goods sold.

_____ 3. (Intro) Cost of products, or merchandise, sold to customers.

_____ 4. (Intro) These decrease assets or increase liabilities but are from peripheral transactions of a business.

_____ 5. (Intro) These arise from consuming resources in order to generate revenue.

_____ 6. (Intro) Sales minus all costs and expenses incurred because of normal operations.

_____ 7. (Intro) These increase assets or decrease liabilities but are from peripheral transactions of a business.

_____ 8. (Intro) Gross sales minus certain items such as sales returns.

Completion

Please write in the word or words which will complete the sentence.

1. (Intro) The ____________________ - ____________________ format of the income statement shows certain subtotals, such as gross margin, for the user.

2. (CO1) The revenue recognition principle states that revenue should be recognized in the accounting records when the earnings process is ______________ ______________ and the amount to be collected is ______________ ______________.

3. (CO2) The ______________ principle governs expense recognition.

4. (CO3) GAAP requires that discontinued operations and extraordinary items appear ______________ ______________ ______________ at the bottom of an income statement.

5. (CO3) If discontinued operations generated a loss for a firm, then the tax effect is called a tax ______________.

6. (CO3) If a company has outstanding 500,000 shares of stock and net income for the period is $100,000, then earnings per share for the period is ______________.

7. (CO4) Common-size income statements, on which each item is divided by net sales and expressed in percentage terms, are used in ______________ analysis.

8. (CO4) The return on shareholders' equity ratio is computed by dividing ______________ ______________ by ______________ ______________ ______________.

Multiple Choice

Please circle the correct answer.

1. (CO4) The ____________ principle states that when acceptable alternatives exist for the accounting treatment of a given transaction, then the one which least overstates assets and income should be selected.
   a. matching
   b. materiality
   c. revenue recognition
   d. conservatism

2. (Intro) The ____________ principle states that separate disclosure is not required if an item is so small that knowledge of it would not affect the decision of a reasonable financial statement reader.
   a. matching
   b. materiality
   c. revenue recognition
   d. conservatism

3. (CO3) The matching principle can be implemented by:
   a. associating cause and effect.
   b. systematic and rational allocation.
   c. immediate recognition.
   d. All of the above are correct.

4. (CO4) Events and transactions that are unusual in nature and infrequent in occurrence are:
   a. extraordinary items.
   b. discontinued operations.
   c. earnings per share.
   d. cost of goods sold.

5. (CO4) Which of the following is an indicator of <u>management's</u> success in operating a firm?
   a. Interest percentage.
   b. Net income percentage.
   c. Operating income percentage.
   d. Income tax percentage.

6. (CO4) Analysis which uses the figures from a prior year's income statement as the base year for calculating percentage increases over a period of time is called:
   a. vertical analysis.
   b. horizontal analysis.
   c. common-size analysis.
   d. gross margin analysis.

7. (CO4) Which of the following ratios divides average total assets into the sum of net income and interest expense (net of tax)?
   a. Times interest earned.
   b. Return on shareholders' equity.
   c. Return on assets.
   d. Earnings per share.

8. (CO4) Which of the following ratios divides interest expense into earnings before interest and taxes?
   a. Times interest earned.
   b. Return on shareholders' equity.
   c. Return on assets.
   d. Earnings per share.

9. (Intro) Which of the following income statements deducts total expenses from total revenues in one simple subtraction?
   a. Multiple-step.
   b. Common-size.
   c. Percentage-of-completion.
   d. Single-step.

10. (Intro) ____________ expense reflects a firm's cost of borrowing money from creditors.
    a. Income tax
    b. Interest
    c. Selling
    d. Administrative

Demonstration Problem

The following are data from the records of Cassandra Company for the year ended June 30, 1998:

Cost of goods sold	$270,000
Utilities expense	9,600
Interest expense	20,000
Office wages expense	56,000
Advertising expense	9,500
Depreciation expense	24,000
Sales salaries expense	76,000
Insurance expense	6,000
Commissions expense	29,000
Sales	975,000
Sales returns	20,000
Hurricane loss (considered extraordinary)	80,000

Assume that the depreciation, utilities, and insurance expenses are split evenly between selling and administrative operations. Assume that the income tax rate is 40%.

REQUIRED:
1. Please prepare in good form a multiple-step income statement. A partial heading is given: Please insert the date (Intro., CO1, CO2, CO3).
2. Please compute earnings per share, rounding if necessary, assuming the number of shares outstanding is 50,000 (CO4).

Cassandra Company
Income Statement

SOLUTIONS TO SELF-TEST

Matching

1. h
2. d
3. a
4. e
5. b
6. g
7. c
8. f

Completion

1. multiple-step
2. substantially complete, reasonably determinable
3. matching
4. net of tax
5. benefit
6. $ .20
7. vertical
8. net income, average shareholders' equity

Multiple Choice

1. d
2. b
3. d
4. a
5. c
6. b
7. c
8. a
9. d
10. b

Demonstration Problem

Cassandra Company
Income Statement
For the Year Ended June 30, 1998

Sales	$975,000		
Less: Sales returns	20,000		
Net sales			$955,000
Cost of goods sold			270,000
Gross margin			$685,000
Selling expenses:			
Advertising expense	$ 9,500		
Sales salaries expense	76,000		
Commissions expense	29,000		
Depreciation expense	12,000		
Utilities expense	4,800		
Insurance expense	3,000		
Total		$134,300	
Administrative expenses:			
Office wages expense	$ 56,000		
Depreciation expense	12,000		
Utilities expense	4,800		
Insurance expense	3,000		
Total		75,800	
Total expenses			210,100
Operating income			$474,900
Interest expense			20,000
			$454,900
Income tax expense			181,960
Net earnings from continuing operations			$272,940
Extraordinary item: Hurricane loss, $80,000 less $32,000 income tax			48,000
Net earnings			$224,940
Earnings per share:			
From continuing operations			$ 5.46
Extraordinary loss			(.96)
Net earnings			$ 4.50

CHAPTER 5

STATEMENT OF CASH FLOWS

CHAPTER OVERVIEW

Chapter 5 examines the statement of cash flows, the fourth formal financial statement. You will learn the purpose of the statement and the three main types of activities included. The direct and the indirect methods of preparing the operating activities section are discussed, and ratios using cash flow information are presented. You will learn how to prepare the operating activities section of the statement.

Review of Specific Chapter Objectives

1. Describe the objectives of the statement of cash flows.

   ▲ The **statement of cash flows** provides information about a firm's inflows and outflows of cash during a period of time. Basically, it states where a firm's money comes from and how it is used. This information is not that easy to find by simply studying the other three financial statements. The statement also explains the change in the Cash account from the beginning to the end of the period.

   ▲ SFAS No. 95, which requires a business to prepare a statement of cash flows, states that the **statement helps readers assess the following:**
   1. A firm's ability to generate positive future net cash flows;
   2. A firm's ability to meet its obligations, its ability to pay dividends, and its needs for external financing;
   3. The reasons for differences between net income and associated cash receipts and payments; and
   4. The effects on a firm's financial position of both its cash and noncash investing and financing transactions.

2. Explain the complementary nature of accrual earnings and cash flows.

- ▲ **Accrual earnings do not necessarily reflect cash flows.** Depreciation expense, for example, reduces accrual net income but is not related at all to cash flow.

- ▲ **Earnings and cash flows should be viewed as complements, not substitutes.** Each has information not necessarily contained in the other. The statement provides information about a firm's liquidity and financial flexibility (the ability to respond to unexpected events by altering the amounts and timing of its cash flows).

- ▲ **A firm must decide whether to focus the statement on cash or on cash and cash equivalents.** Cash equivalents are short-term, highly liquid financial instruments with maturities of less than months. Examples include money market funds, treasury bills, and certificates of deposit (CDs).

3. Identify the three types of activities that generate and use cash.

- ▲ **Operating activities** involve transactions related to providing goods and services to customers. They show the cash flow effects of the typical transactions which appear on the income statement. Examples include receipt of payment from customers and payments to employees and suppliers.

- ▲ **Investing activities** usually involve cash flows from the acquisition and disposal of noncurrent assets. Examples include the purchase or sale of property, plant, and equipment and the purchase or sale of investments in other corporations.

- ▲ **Financing activities** include cash flows from obtaining and repaying financing. This includes transactions involving long-term liabilities and shareholders' equity. Examples include payment of dividends and buying back shares from shareholders.

4. Explain the difference between the direct and the indirect methods of presenting a statement of cash flows.

- ▲ **SFAS No. 95 allows two methods for preparation of the operating activities section of the statement of cash flows: the direct and the indirect methods.**

- ▲ Under the **direct method**, a separate line item is provided for each type of operating cash inflow and outflow. These line items correspond to categories on the income statement. A **major advantage of this method** is that the primary sources and uses of cash are listed.

▲ The **indirect method** begins with accrual-basis net income and makes adjustments to it in order to arrive at cash generated by operating activities. A **major advantage of this method** is that the reasons for the difference between net income and cash generated by operations are detailed.

▲ While **the FASB prefers the direct method**, businesses use the indirect method more frequently for two reasons: 1) The indirect approach is similar to the approach used for preparation of the statement required before the issuance of SFAS No. 95; and 2) a firm using the direct approach must provide a schedule that reconciles net income with cash provided by operating activities (this schedule consists of the information contained in the indirect approach).

▲ **Noncash investing and financing activities do not appear in the body of the statement** but are summarized in a schedule that appears at the end of the statement. Examples of such activities include the purchase of land by issuing common stock or the purchase of equipment by issuing a note payable.

5. Draw inferences about the financial performance of a firm from the statement of cash flows.

▲ **Creditors, shareholders, and analysts find the statement's operating activities section to be very useful.** Many analysts prefer operating activities to net income as a performance measure because net income can be manipulated by accounting conventions.

▲ A variety of **ratios can be computed using the operating activities section. Cash return on assets** is calculated by dividing average total assets into the sum of cash flow from operating activities (CFOA), interest paid, and taxes paid. This ratio measures management's success in generating cash from operating activities, and a high ratio is desirable. Some analysts use free cash flow instead of CFOA. Free cash flow is calculated by subtracting from CFOA the cash payment necessary to replace worn-out equipment.

▲ The **quality of sales ratio** is computed by dividing sales into cash received from customers. **Cash received from customers** can be computed by adding the beginning balance of accounts receivable and sales and then subtracting the ending balance of accounts receivable. This ratio is useful in analyzing firms that use liberal revenue recognition policies or firms which must exercise considerable judgment in selecting revenue recognition policies. This ratio can reflect a firm's performance in collecting from customers. A high ratio is desirable.

▲ The **quality of income ratio** is computed by dividing net income into CFOA. This ratio indicates the proportion of income which has been realized in cash, and high levels of the ratio are desirable. The ratio often exceeds 100%.

- ▲ The **cash interest coverage ratio** is computed by adding CFOA and interest and tax payments and then dividing the total by interest payments. It is used by creditors to assess a firm's ability to pay interest. As is true with the three ratios discussed above, a high ratio is desirable.

- ▲ **The statement's investing and financing activities sections are scrutinized less closely by financial statement users.**

6. Calculate cash flow from operating activities by using relationships among income statement and balance sheet items.

- ▲ **To determine cash flows from operating activities using the direct method, the following are computed:**

  Cash collections from customers =
  Beginning Accts. Rec. + Sales - Ending Accts. Rec.

  Interest received =
  Beginning Int. Rec. + Int. Revenue - Ending Int. Rec.

  Payments to employees =
  Beginning Sal. Payable + Sal. Exp. - Ending Sal. Payable

  Payments to suppliers =
  Beginning Acct. Pay. + Purchases - Ending Acct. Payable
  To solve for Purchases, remember how to solve for Cost of Goods Sold: COGS = Beginning Inv. + Purchases - Ending Inv. Rearrange the equation to solve for Purchases: Purchases = COGS - Beginning Inventory + Ending Inventory.

  Interest paid =
  Beginning Int. Pay. + Int. Expense - Ending Int. Pay.

- ▲ **Depreciation expense is not considered when using the direct method.**

- ▲ **Do not consider gains and losses associated with nonoperating activities.**

- ▲ **Adjust remaining income statement items by the changes in related balance sheet accounts.**

- ▲ When **using the indirect approach,** accrual-basis net income is converted to cash flows from operating activities. Expense items, such as depreciation, which have reduced net income must be added back because they do not involve cash flow. Other items, such as Accounts Receivable, must be addressed.

If Accounts Receivable has increased during the period, then the increase must be deducted from accrual-basis net income because this indicates that credit sales, which do not involve cash flow, have increased the net income number. The opposite will be true if Accounts Receivable has decreased during the period.

▲ **The investing and financing activities sections will be exactly the same under both the direct and the indirect methods.**

CHAPTER SELF-TEST

Note: The notation (CO1) means that the question was drawn from chapter objective number one.

Matching

Please write the letters of the following terms in the spaces to the left of the definitions.

a. Cash equivalents
b. Direct approach
c. Financing activities
d. Indirect approach
e. Investing activities
f. Operating activities

_____ 1. (CO3) Activities typically involving transactions related to providing goods and services to customers.

_____ 2. (CO2) Short-term, highly liquid financial instruments with maturities of less than three months.

_____ 3. (CO3) Activities which include cash flows from obtaining and repaying financing.

_____ 4. (CO4) Under this method, a separate line item is provided for each type of operating cash inflow and outflow.

_____ 5. (CO3) Activities which involve cash flows from the acquisition and disposal of noncurrent assets.

_____ 6. (CO4) Under this method, adjustments are made to net income in order to arrive at cash generated by operating activities.

Completion

Please write in the word or words which will complete the sentence.

1. (CO4) Cash collections from customers and payments to employees need to be computed when an accountant prepares the operating activities section of the statement of cash flows using the ____________________ approach.

2. (CO4) A major advantage of the ____________________ method is that the reasons for the difference between net income and cash generated by operations are detailed.

3. (CO4) The purchase of a piece of equipment by the issuance of common stock is an example of a __________ __________ __________ __________ activity.

4. (CO5) The __________ __________ __________ ratio is computed by dividing sales into cash received from customers.

5. (CO5) A ____________________ level of the quality of income ratio is desirable.

6. (CO4) Under the ____________________ approach, depreciation expense is added to accrual-basis net income.

7. (CO1) The statement of cash flows provides information about a firm's ____________ and ____________ of cash during a period of time.

8. (CO6) Cash collections from customers is computing by ____________________ the beginning balance in Accounts Receivable to Sales and ____________________ the ending balance in Accounts Receivable.

Multiple Choice

Please circle the correct answer.

1. (CO3) The payment of dividends to a corporation's shareholders is an example of a/an __________ activity.
   a. operating
   b. investing
   c. financing
   d. noncash investing and financing

2. (CO3) Selling a piece of equipment for cash is an example of a/an ____________ activity.
   a. operating
   b. investing
   c. financing
   d. noncash investing and financing

3. (CO5) If average total assets is divided into the sum of cash flow from operating activities, interest paid, and taxes paid, then the result is the ____________ ratio.
   a. cash return on assets
   b. quality of sales
   c. quality of income
   d. cash interest coverage

4. (CO5) If net income is divided into cash flow from operating activities, then the result is the ____________ ratio.
   a. cash return on assets
   b. quality of sales
   c. quality of income
   d. cash interest coverage

5. (CO6) If an accountant is preparing the operating activities section of the statement of cash flows using the indirect method, depreciation expense is:
   a. ignored.
   b. deducted from net income.
   c. added to net income.
   d. None of the above is correct. Depreciation expense is included in the investing activities section.

6. (CO6) Beginning Interest Receivable is $500, Interest Revenue is $1,000, and ending Interest Receivable is $250. The dollar amount of interest received, using the direct approach for the operating activities section, is:
   a. $1,750.
   b. $1,250.
   c. $1,000.
   d. $ 750.

7. (CO6) Beginning inventory is $2,000, ending inventory is $1,500, and cost of goods sold is $3,000. Beginning Accounts Payable is $4,000, and ending Accounts Payable is $3,000. The dollar amount paid to suppliers, using the direct approach for the operating activities section, is:
   a. $4,000.
   b. $3,500.
   c. $2,500.
   d. $1,500.

8. (CO6) If an accountant is preparing the operating activities section of the statement of cash flows using the indirect method, a decrease in accounts payable is:
   a. deducted from net income.
   b. added to net income.
   c. ignored.
   d. None of the above is correct. Analysis of accounts payable is included in the financing activities section.

9. (CO5) The ____________ ratio is used by creditors to assess a firm's ability to pay interest.
   a. cash return on assets
   b. quality of sales
   c. quality of income
   d. cash interest coverage

10. (CO3) Receipt of cash from customers and payments to suppliers are examples of ____________ activities.
   a. operating
   b. investing
   c. financing
   d. noncash investing and financing

Demonstration Problem

Please indicate whether the following transactions of Pooky Corporation are operating (O) activities, investing (I) activities, financing (F) activities, or noncash (NC) investing or financing activities (CO3).

1. Merchandise inventory was sold on account to customers.
2. The company repurchased some of its common stock.
3. The company paid three of its suppliers.
4. A piece of land was purchased for cash.
5. Pooky issued 4,000 shares of common stock for the purchase of a building.
6. To raise money, the company sold bonds with a value of $5,000,000.
7. The corporation paid the first interest payment on the bonds.
8. The company sold a building for cash.
9. The company recorded a $150,000 gain on the sale of the building in number 8.
10. Several of the customers from number 1 paid the company.
11. Several long-term investments were sold by the company.
12. The company paid a dividend to its shareholders.
13. The corporation sold 5,000 shares of common stock and received cash.
14. A new piece of equipment was purchased by the issuance of a long-term note payable.
15. The company recorded its annual depreciation.

SOLUTIONS TO SELF-TEST

Matching

1. f
2. a
3. c
4. b
5. e
6. d

Completion

1. direct
2. indirect
3. noncash investing and financing
4. quality of sales
5. high
6. indirect
7. inflows, outflows
8. adding, subtracting

Multiple Choice

1. c
2. b
3. a
4. c
5. c
6. b
7. b
8. a
9. d
10. a

Demonstration Problem

1. O
2. F
3. O
4. I
5. NC
6. F
7. O
8. I
9. O
10. O
11. I
12. F
13. F
14. NC
15. NC

CHAPTER 6

CURRENT ASSETS

CHAPTER OVERVIEW

Chapter 6 examines the current assets section of the balance sheet. You will learn about cash, marketable securities, accounts receivable, inventories, and prepaid expenses. In the appendix, you will learn how to prepare one type of bank reconciliation.

Review of Specific Chapter Objectives

1. Identify the items included in cash.

   ▲ **Cash is listed first in the current assets section** because it is the most liquid of the assets. Remember from chapter 3 that liquidity reflects the ability of a firm to generate sufficient cash to meet its operating cash needs and to pay its obligations as they become due.

   ▲ **A company must be careful to have on hand enough cash to pay its bills but not so much that cash is sitting idle.** It also must have internal controls in place to safeguard cash.

   ▲ **Cash is composed of funds that are readily available.** It includes cash on hand, cash on deposit in checking accounts and saving accounts, money market funds permitting withdrawal by check, checks from customers awaiting deposit, and foreign currency which can be converted into dollars.

   ▲ **Cash does not include certificates of deposit, stamps, and post-dated checks.** A post-dated check is a check written, for example, on July 6 but dated July 8. Because the bank should not accept this check until July 8, the check should be classified not as cash but as an account receivable.

- ▲ **Cash is usually reported as one item on the balance sheet.** If a company has several checking accounts, then they are combined into one number. The same is true for petty cash funds, funds kept to pay for small, incidental expenditures, and change funds, which enable cashiers to make change for their customers.

- ▲ **When borrowing from banks, firms sometimes agree to maintain compensating balances,** which are minimum amounts the firm agrees to keep on deposit at the bank in accounts that pay little or no interest. These balances effectively raise the interest rate that the bank is charging the borrowing company. Compensating balances are included in the Cash number and disclosed in the notes to the financial statements.

- ▲ Some companies choose to report the first item on the balance sheet as **Cash and Cash Equivalents** which, as you remember from chapter 5, are short-term, highly liquid investments with a maturity date of less than three months. Examples of cash equivalents are certificates of deposit, treasury bills, and commercial paper.

2. Appreciate the need for cash planning and how firms exercise control over cash.

- ▲ **Because cash is highly liquid and universally desirable, it behooves a company to have tight internal controls over cash.**

- ▲ **Employees who have control over the cash itself should have nothing to do with the recordkeeping for cash.** This is called separation of duties. A person who has custody and does the recordkeeping has an excellent opportunity to steal from the company.

- ▲ **Bank checking accounts provide several control advantages. First,** cash receipts can be deposited daily, critically important since the longer cash stays at a place of business, the higher the chances that it will be stolen. **Second,** checks provide a written record of a firm's disbursements. **Third,** since only a few individuals will have check-signing authority, the company restricts access to cash and reduces the possibility that it will be used improperly. **Fourth,** bank statements provide a monthly listing of deposits and withdrawals.

- ▲ While the statement of cash flows analyzes a firm's inflows and outflows of cash, **the balance sheet simply gives a total for Cash as of a given date.** A severe test of liquidity is performed by dividing current liabilities into Cash. Recall that the current and acid-test ratios also have current liabilities in the denominator; the numerator, however, is all current assets for the former and cash, marketable securities, and net accounts receivable for the latter.

▲ **Managers must be proactive in ensuring that enough cash is on hand to meet current obligations.** To accomplish this, management must project the amount and timing of future cash flows.

3. Comprehend the basic accounting for marketable securities and the limitations of generally accepted accounting principles in this area.

▲ **Marketable securities are the next current asset in order of liquidity.** These consist of stocks and bonds easily sold through a broker. A security is considered marketable if it is traded on an exchange registered with the SEC or if its price is available through the National Association of Securities Dealers Automated Quotations (NASDAQ) systems or the National Quotation Bureau.

▲ There are **two general types of securities:** equity securities, which represent ownership interests in other corporations, and debt securities, which are evidence of lending transactions. Equity securities basically mean stocks, while debt securities basically mean bonds or other commercial paper.

▲ **SFAS No. 115 requires that a business classify its short-term equity securities as either trading securities or available-for-sale securities.** Trading securities are intended to be held for a short period of time. The available-for-sale securities category covers all other equity securities.

▲ **Equity available-for-sale securities must be stated at their market value on the balance sheet date.** Please note that this is a departure from the historical cost rule that you have learned. Any difference between the cost and the market value is an unrealized gain or loss. The word "unrealized" means that a transaction has not actually taken place: The gain or loss is only a "paper" gain or loss. Unrealized gains or losses do NOT appear on the income statement: They are put into a special section of shareholders' equity. A gain will increase equity, while a loss will decrease equity. The adjustment to market value is made to a valuation account, often called Allowance for Unrealized Gain/Loss. Suppose that securities are purchased for $5,000, but at the balance sheet date, the market value is only $4,300. Two accounts must be created. An Allowance account is created for $700, and the current assets section of the balance sheet will show the following:

Available-for-Sale Securities	$5,000
Less: Allowance for Unrealized Gain/Loss	700
Available-for-Sale Securities, at Market Value	$4,300

This presentation should remind you of the manner in which property, plant, and equipment assets are presented: The cost of the asset less the Accumulated Depreciation account yields the book value of the asset.

The second account created, Unrealized Loss on Marketable Securities, will appear with its $700 balance in the shareholders' equity section of the balance sheet, not on the income statement.

▲ When **securities are sold**, gains or losses on the sale are realized. The word "realized" means that a transaction has actually taken place. If the securities mentioned above are sold for $4,800, then there is a $200 realized loss ($5,000 cost - $4,800 cash received). If they are sold for $5,400, then there is a $400 realized gain ($5,400 cash received - $5,000 cost). The entry which recorded the $700 unrealized loss must be reversed off the books.

▲ **Equity trading securities**, which are intended to be held for a short period of time, are also accounted for at market value. They follow the same accounting as mentioned above for available-for-sale securities with one notable exception: Unrealized gains and losses ARE included in net income on the income statement.

▲ **The accounting for debt securities is more complex.** If a firm intends to hold a debt security until the maturity date, the security is valued at historical cost. Otherwise, the securities appear on the balance sheet at market value.

▲ In summation, **marketable securities are reflected on the balance sheet at market value.** The amount of cash for which marketable securities can be exchanged is likely to be more relevant for liquidity assessment than is the historical cost of the securities.

4. Determine if a firm is properly managing its accounts receivable.

▲ **Accounts receivable, the next most liquid current asset, arise when a firm sells on credit to customers.** It is critically important that a firm assess the credit-worthiness of a customer before it extends credit to that customer.

Deciding to whom to grant credit and how much credit to grant are extremely important decisions for a business.

▲ **When a firm sells goods on credit to a customer, revenue is recognized at the time of sale,** despite the fact that cash will not be received until a later date.

▲ **Firms often offer cash discounts to customers** to entice the customers to pay early. This gives the firm earlier access to cash and helps to minimize the chances that the account will not be paid. If terms are listed as "1/10, n/15," then this means that a 1% discount will be given if the account is paid within 10 days. Otherwise, the entire bill is due in 15 days.

▲ **Firms can also sell accounts receivable to factors,** institutions which buy accounts receivable. If a business sells $10,000 worth of accounts receivable, however, then it will not receive the full $10,000. There will be a financing expense to compensate the factor for the cost of collection, the delayed receipt of cash, and potential uncollectible accounts.

▲ **Companies know that, even under the best circumstances, they will not collect on all their receivables,** and they make a year-end adjustment for the amount deemed uncollectible. This amount is an estimate: The company does not know at this time which customers will not pay their bills. An expense, often called Uncollectible Accounts Expense, is created, as is an account called Allowance for Uncollectible Accounts, a contra-asset account. The balance sheet presentation for gross receivables of $5,000 and an Allowance account of $400 is:

Accounts Receivable, Gross	$5,000
Less: Allowance for Uncollectible Accounts	400
Accounts Receivable, Net	$4,600

Please note that this presentation is similar to that of the available-for-sale securities noted above.

▲ **When the company knows that a specific account receivable is not likely to be paid, it must write that receivable off the books.** This is accomplished by reducing both the account receivable and the allowance account. It is interesting to note that the net accounts receivable number is exactly the same before and after the write-off.

▲ **One method for estimating the number for the year-end**

adjustment is the aging method. Accounts receivable are classified as current and past due: Each category is assigned a percentage of uncollectibility, with the past due's being higher than the current's. The longer the bill is unpaid, the higher the chance that it will never be paid. The percentage is based upon a firm's past experience, industry standards, and current trends.

▲ The **analysis of accounts receivable involves two issues:** the relative size of accounts receivable and the adequacy of the allowance for uncollectible accounts. **Accounts receivable as a percentage of sales** is computed by dividing sales (net credit) into gross accounts receivable. The **collection period,** which indicates the number of days' sales in accounts receivable, can be computed by dividing average sales per day into gross accounts receivable. (Average sales per day is computed by dividing 365 into sales.)

5. Assess if a firm's allowance for uncollectible accounts is adequate.

▲ The **adequacy of the Allowance account** is usually assessed relative to the year-end balance of accounts receivable. This is calculated by dividing gross accounts receivable into the Allowance for Uncollectible Accounts.

▲ **Managers should be aware that credit must be managed at both the beginning and the end of the process.** Certainly the firm must be careful about the customers to whom it grants credit, and then it must be careful about its collection policies. It must be vigilant that monies owed to it are paid within the agreed-upon period.

6. Understand the various inventory cost flow assumptions and the effect that the firm's choice of inventory method has on its taxes, the quality of information in the financial statements, its management compensation, its loan covenants, and its stock price.

▲ **Inventory is often the largest current asset of a firm.** It consists of products acquired for resale to customers.

▲ Please remember from chapter 4 that the **difference between sales and the cost of goods sold** is called gross profit or gross margin.

▲ Please also remember the following:

Beginning inventory
+ Purchases
___
Cost of goods available for sale
- Ending inventory
___
Cost of goods sold

▲ The **physical flow of most types of goods** is that the oldest goods are sold first. Consider a grocery store's produce department. Certainly the store wants to sell the lettuce it receives on Monday before the lettuce it receives on Friday because of the perishability of the lettuce. The same is true of staple goods even though they have longer shelf lives.

▲ Despite the actual physical flow of goods, there are **several cost flow assumptions** used in assigning a cost to the ending inventory and to cost of goods sold. One of these is specific identification, used when a firm sells low-volume, high-cost items. This method is appropriate for a car dealer or a jewelry store, but it would be horrendous for a retailer like Wal-Mart. The firm maintains accounting records showing the cost of each inventory item, making it easy to determine what has been sold and what is still left on hand at the end of the accounting period.

▲ Another cost flow assumption is **average cost**. Despite the number of purchases made throughout the period, an average cost of items is computed by dividing the number of units available for sale into the cost of goods available for sale. The average cost thus computed is then multiplied by the number of units sold to give the cost of goods sold and by the number of units left to give the value of the ending inventory. Please note that the cost of goods available for sale consists of costs of the beginning inventory plus the cost of all purchases made during a period. Students often forget to add in the beginning inventory. If the cost of goods available for sale is $10,000 and the number of units available for sale is 1,000, then the average cost per unit is $10.00. If 600 units are sold, then the cost of goods sold is $6,000 ($10 X 600 units). The ending inventory will be $4,000 ($10 X 400 units still on hand). **If you know the cost of goods available for sale and either cost of goods sold or ending inventory, then it is easy to compute the other by subtracting it from the cost of goods available for sale.**

▲ Another cost flow assumption is **first-in, first-out** (or **FIFO**). It follows the physical flow of goods in that it assumes that oldest goods on hand are the first sold. The beginning inventory and the earliest purchases are assumed to be sold first, thus being part of cost of goods sold, while the cost of the most recent purchases will be assigned to ending inventory.

▲ A final cost flow assumption is **last-in, first-out (or LIFO)**. The most recent purchases are assumed to have been sold, thus being part of cost of goods sold, while the cost of the beginning inventory and the oldest purchases will be assigned to ending inventory.

▲ **Choice of inventory method can have significant effects on both the income statement and the balance sheet.** Assume a period of rising prices. LIFO will give the highest cost of goods sold and lowest net income and the lowest value for inventory on the balance sheet. FIFO will give the lowest cost of goods sold and highest net income and the highest value for inventory on the balance sheet. The opposite, of course, will be true if the firm enters a period of falling prices. Average cost numbers will fall between FIFO and LIFO numbers.

▲ **All of the above methods are acceptable for GAAP.**

▲ With respect to **taxes**, LIFO gives the lowest taxable income, thus increasing a firm's cash flow. If a firm uses LIFO for tax purposes, then it must be used for financial reporting. FIFO will give the highest taxable income.

▲ **LIFO is more costly to implement than either FIFO or average cost.**

▲ With respect to **quality of financial statement information**, please be aware that there is usually a trade-off between the income statement and the balance sheet. One will have pretty accurate numbers while the other will be a little off. This is acceptable and understood in the financial accounting community. LIFO will provide fairly accurate cost of goods sold information but will understate ending inventory on the balance sheet. FIFO will provide fairly accurate ending inventory information but will understate cost of goods sold. These differences make it clear that it is **critical for a business to disclose in the notes to the financial statements which inventory methods it uses.**

▲ With respect to the **current ratio and loan agreements**, LIFO gives a lower number for ending inventory, thus lowering the numerator for the current ratio.

▲ With respect to **management compensation**, since LIFO leads to lower net income, managers whose bonuses are tied to net income might be motivated not to use LIFO.

- ▲ With respect to **stock prices**, the best evidence available suggests that the stock market responds favorably to LIFO adoptions.

- ▲ **Generally accepted accounting principles require** that inventories be valued at the lower of cost or market (LCM). Market is defined as replacement cost. This is based on the rationale that a decline in replacement cost indicates that the inventory's utility to the firm has decreased. If inventory cost $50,000 but at the end of the accounting period has a replacement cost of $48,000, then the inventory must be reported on the balance sheet at $48,000. If that same inventory has a replacement cost of $53,000, then it must be reported at $50,000.

- ▲ **Manufacturers** usually have three categories of inventory. **Raw materials** are the goods which go into the manufacture of a company's products. **Work-in-process** consists of products which have been started but not finished at the balance sheet date. **Finished goods** are those items which have been completed but not yet sold.

7. Analyze a firm's inventory management practices.

- ▲ It is **useful to compute the gross profit percentage**, dividing sales into gross profit. A higher gross profit percentage helps cover other expenses and contributes to net income.

- ▲ **Inadequate levels of inventory** may result in lost sales and reduced profitability. **Excessive levels of inventory** increase carrying costs, which include storage, handling, insurance, and the opportunity cost on the funds invested in inventory.

- ▲ The **number of days sales in ending inventory** is computed by dividing cost of goods sold per day into ending inventory. (Cost of goods sold per day is computed by dividing 365 into cost of goods sold.)

- ▲ **Companies using LIFO often reveal their FIFO-based net income and inventory values.**

8. Appreciate the importance of prepaid expenses.

- ▲ The **last current asset, the least liquid,** is prepaid expenses. Rent and insurance are examples. When rent is paid or an insurance policy purchased, the firm has purchased an asset. As time elapses, the asset is used up, and its cost becomes an expense.

- ▲ These assets are **not expected to be converted into cash:** The asset purchased is expected to be consumed. The prepaids are generally a very small portion of a firm's current assets.

9. Appendix: Prepare a bank reconciliation.

- ▲ **Rarely does the ending balance on a bank statement equal the amount shown in a checking account.** Reasons for the difference include timing differences and errors.

- ▲ Examples of **items known to the company but not showing on the bank statement** include deposits-in-transit and outstanding checks. A **deposit-in-transit** is a deposit showing on the firm's books but not yet added to the company's account in the bank system. An **outstanding check** is one which has been deducted from company records but not yet deducted from the bank account.

- ▲ Examples of **items known to the bank but not to the company until it receives its bank statement** include bank service charges and preauthorized withdrawals. The company may know that it will have a service charge but will not know the amount until it receives the bank statement.

- ▲ **Errors** can be made either in the accounting records or on the bank statement.

- ▲ **One form of bank reconciliation involves adjusting the ending bank balance and the book balance to a corrected balance.** A deposit-in-transit will always be an addition to the bank side of the reconciliation. An outstanding check will always be a subtraction from the bank side. A bank service charge will always be a subtraction from the company side of the reconciliation, as will a preauthorized withdrawal. Errors must be analyzed to see what side of the reconciliation they affect.

CHAPTER SELF-TEST

Note: The notation (CO1) means that the question was drawn from chapter objective number one.

Matching

Please write the letters of the following terms in the spaces to the left of the definitions.

a. Accounts receivable
b. Debt securities
c. Equity securities
d. FIFO
e. Inventories
f. LIFO
g. Prepaid expenses

_____ 1. (CO3) Securities which are evidence of lending transactions: Examples are commercial paper and bonds.

_____ 2. (CO6) Method which assumes that the most recent purchases have been sold.

_____ 3. (CO4) Third most liquid current asset.

_____ 4. (CO6) Method which assumes that the most recent purchases remain in ending inventory.

_____ 5. (CO3) Assets, the cost of which becomes an expense as the asset is consumed: An example is rent.

_____ 6. (CO3) Securities which represent ownership interests in other corporations.

_____ 7. (CO6) Products acquired for resale to customers.

Completion

Please write in the word or words which will complete the sentence.

1. (CO6) The ______________________ inventory method assumes that the beginning inventory and oldest purchases have been sold during the accounting period.

2. (CO1) As part of borrowing agreements with banks, firms sometimes agree to maintain ______________________ ______________________, minimum amounts the firm agrees to keep on deposit at the lending bank.

3. (CO3) Equity securities can be classified either as available-for-sale or ________________________.

4. (CO3) Marketable equity securities are reported at their ________________________ ________________________ on the balance sheet date.

5. (CO4) In order to obtain cash more quickly, firms sometimes ________________________ their receivables.

6. (CO4) If a firm's net accounts receivable is $15,000 before a write-off of $1,000, then the net accounts receivable is ________________________ after the write-off.

7. (CO6) The total of beginning inventory and purchases gives ____.

8. (CO6) In a period of rising prices, ________________________ gives the highest cost of goods sold and the lowest net income.

9. (CO7) ________________________ costs include storage, handling, insurance, and the opportunity cost on the funds invested in inventory.

10. (App.) ____________________ ____________________ are always deducted from the bank side of a bank reconciliation.

<u>Multiple Choice</u>

Please circle the correct answer.

1. (CO2) Which of the following statements is correct?
   a. An employee who handles cash should also do the record-keeping for cash.
   b. An employee who handles cash should not do the record-keeping for cash.
   c. A retail clerk should read the daily sales total from the cash register and then record this amount in the accounting records.
   d. Cash should be deposited in the bank account every two weeks.

2. (CO1) Which of the following is considered to be cash?
   a. Post-dated checks.
   b. Postage stamps.
   c. Certificates of deposit.
   d. Money in a savings account.

3. (CO1) Small, incidental expenditures of a firm should be paid out of a:
   a. checking account.
   b. savings account.
   c. petty cash fund.
   d. change fund.

4. (CO3) Unrealized gains or losses on available-for-sale equity securities should appear:
   a. in a special section of shareholders' equity on the balance sheet.
   b. on the income statement.
   c. in a special section of assets on the balance sheet.
   d. on the statement of shareholders' equity.

5. (CO4) The proper presentation of accounts receivable on the balance sheet shows:
   a. accounts receivable plus the Allowance for Uncollectible Accounts.
   b. accounts receivable less the Allowance for Uncollectible Accounts.
   c. gross accounts receivable, with no consideration given to the Allowance for Uncollectible Accounts.
   d. None of the above is correct.

6. (CO4) The year-end adjustment for accounts receivable involves:
   a. a decrease in Uncollectible Accounts Expense and a decrease in Allowance for Uncollectible Accounts.
   b. a decrease in Uncollectible Accounts Expense and an increase in Allowance for Uncollectible Accounts.
   c. an increase in Uncollectible Accounts Expense and an increase in Allowance for Uncollectible Accounts.
   d. an increase in Uncollectible Accounts Expense and a decrease in Allowance for Uncollectible Accounts.

7. (CO6) Beginning inventory consisted of 100 units at a total cost of $500. Total purchases were 900 units at a total cost of $5,400. Units sold totaled 800. The dollar amount of ending inventory, using the average-cost method, is:
   a. $4,800.
   b. $4,720.
   c. $1,200.
   d. $1,180.

8. (CO6) A manufacturer's inventories consist of:
   a. raw materials and finished goods only.
   b. work-in-process and finished goods only.
   c. raw materials, work-in-process, and finished goods.
   d. raw materials and work-in-process only.

9. (App) Which of the following is subtracted from the book side of a bank reconciliation?
   a. Bank service charge.
   b. Outstanding checks.
   c. Deposits-in-transit.
   d. None of the above is correct.

10. (App) The ending balance on the bank statement is $2,512. Outstanding checks total $1,100, while there is one deposit-in-transit totaling $500. The bank service charge is $13. On the bank reconciliation, the corrected balance will be:
   a. $3,112.
   b. $1,912.
   c. $1,899.
   d. $1,399.

Demonstration Problem

The accounting records of New River Corporation show the following data for 1998:

Date	Units Purchased	Unit Price
1- 5	300	$7.00
4-15	600	7.10
8-22	500	7.25
11-30	700	7.40

Inventory on hand at the beginning of 1998 consisted of 200 units with a unit price of $7.00 During the accounting period, 2,100 units were sold.

REQUIRED:

1. Please calculate ending inventory and cost of goods sold using FIFO, LIFO, and average cost (CO6).
2. If all the units were sold for $15.00, then what is the gross profit under FIFO, LIFO, and average cost (CO6)?
3. What is the number of days sales in ending inventory using FIFO (CO7)?

1.

2.

3.

SOLUTIONS TO SELF-TEST

Matching

1. b
2. f
3. a
4. d
5. g
6. c
7. e

Completion

1. FIFO
2. compensating balances
3. trading
4. market value
5. factor
6. $15,000
7. cost of goods available for sale
8. LIFO
9. Carrying
10. Outstanding checks

Multiple Choice

1. b
2. d
3. c
4. a
5. b
6. c
7. d
8. c
9. a
10. b

Demonstration Problem

1.

Date	Units Purchased	Unit Price	Total Cost
Bal.	200	$7.00	$ 1,400
1- 5	300	7.00	2,100
4-15	600	7.10	4,260
8-22	500	7.25	3,625
11-30	700	7.40	5,180
Cost of goods available for sale			$16,565

FIFO Ending inventory 200 X $7.40 = $1,480

Cost of goods sold

200 X $7.00 =	$ 1,400
300 X $7.00 =	2,100
600 X $7.10 =	4,260
500 X $7.25 =	3,625
500 X $7.40 =	3,700
2,100	$15,085

OR $16,565 - $1,480 = $15,085

LIFO Ending inventory 200 X $7.00 = $1,400

(Note that these are the 200 units from beginning inventory.)

Cost of goods sold

700 X $7.40 =	$ 5,180
500 X $7.25 =	3,625
600 X $7.10 =	4,260
300 X $7.00 =	2,100
2,100	$15,165

OR $16,565 - $1,400 = $15,165

Average Cost $16,565 ÷ 2,300 units = $7.20 per unit (rounded)

Ending inventory 200 X $7.20 = $1,440

Cost of goods sold 2,100 X $7.20 = $15,120

(If the two are added, then the total is $16,560. The $5.00 difference is due to the rounding performed when computing average unit cost.)

(Note that the average cost numbers fall between the FIFO and the LIFO numbers.)

2. Sales are $31,500 (2,100 X $15.00).

	FIFO	Aver. Cost	LIFO
Sales	$31,500	$31,500	$31,500
Less: COGS	15,085	15,120	15,165
Gross margin	$16,415	$16,380	$16,335

3. CGS per day = CGS ÷ 365

$15,085 ÷ 365 = $41.33 (rounded)

NDS = Ending inventory ÷ CGS per day

$1,480 ÷ $41.33 = 35.81 days

CHAPTER 7

NONCURRENT ASSETS

CHAPTER OVERVIEW

Chapter 7 examines the noncurrent assets section of the balance sheet. You will learn about property, plant, and equipment assets, intangible assets, and natural resources. You will learn how to account for their initial acquisition and methods for depreciation, amortization, and depletion. The accounting for post-acquisition expenditures will be discussed, as will the accounting for write-downs and disposals.

Review of Specific Chapter Objectives

1. Identify three major types of noncurrent assets: (1) property, plant, and equipment, (2) intangible assets, and (3) natural resources. **THIS SECTION WILL DISCUSS PROPERTY, PLANT, AND EQUIPMENT.**

   ▲ **Noncurrent assets are long-lived assets**, not expected to be fully utilized within one year.

   ▲ **Property, plant, and equipment (PPE)**, also called fixed assets, are <u>tangible, long-lived assets used by a firm which derive value from their physical substance</u>. Examples include land, land improvements, office buildings, office equipment, manufacturing facilities, and factory equipment.

2. Explain how to account for the acquisition of these assets. **THIS SECTION WILL DISCUSS PROPERTY, PLANT, AND EQUIPMENT.**

   ▲ **Property, plant, and equipment** are <u>initially valued at their historical cost</u>. This includes <u>all costs necessary to acquire the asset and to get the asset in location and condition for use</u>. Therefore, invoice price (less discounts), sales taxes, transportation charges, installation costs, costs of trial runs, and costs to refurbish equipment purchased used are included in the cost of the asset.

▲ When an accountant says that a **cost has been capitalized**, he or she means that it has increased an asset account.

3. Describe the procedures for depreciation, amortization, and depletion. **THIS SECTION WILL DISCUSS DEPRECIATION.**

▲ **Depreciation** is the process of allocating the cost of a fixed asset to an expense in the years that the asset helps generate revenue. It is an **application of the matching principle.** Of the property, plant, and equipment assets, land alone is not depreciated. A purchaser of land hopes that its value will appreciate instead.

▲ **GAAP permits use of any systematic, rational method of depreciation.** Three methods are discussed here: straight-line, sum-of-the-years'-digits, and declining-balance.

▲ **Straight-line depreciation** assumes that depreciation is a function of time. Once depreciation expense is calculated, the same amount will be taken each year. To compute straight-line depreciation expense, the following formula is used:

(Historical cost - Residual Value) ÷ Number of years

Residual value is the amount a firm expects to receive from selling the asset at the end of its useful economic life. Both it and the number of years are estimates. When the residual value is subtracted from the historical cost, the resulting difference is called the depreciable base.

▲ **When depreciation is recorded,** an expense is increased, as is an account called Accumulated Depreciation. The latter account is called a contra-asset account. The **balance sheet presentation of a depreciable asset** is as follows:

Asset
Less: Accumulated Depreciation

Book Value

▲ If an asset costs $110,000 and has a residual value of $5,000 and an estimated useful life of 5 years, then the annual depreciation will be $21,000 per year [($110,000 - $5,000) ÷ 5 years]. Total depreciation expense over the 5-year life of the asset will be $105,000. When the asset is fully depreciated, the balance sheet will show the following:

Asset	$110,000
Less: Accum. Depreciation	105,000
Book Value	$ 5,000

Note that the **book value equals the residual value when the asset has been fully depreciated.**

▲ **Sum-of-the-years'-digits depreciation** is one of the so-called accelerated methods of depreciation. More depreciation is taken in the early years of the asset's life, when the asset is more productive. In the later years of the asset's life, as productivity falls off, depreciation will be lower; however, maintenance and repairs expense will probably be higher.

▲ Just as is true for straight-line depreciation, the **computation for sum-of-the-years'-digits starts with the depreciable base.** This number is multiplied by a fraction. The **denominator** is the sum of the years' digits (for a 5-year useful life, 5 + 4 + 3 + 2 + 1, or 15), while the **numerator** is the largest of the available numbers, 1, 2, 3, 4, or 5. Remember that this is an accelerated method, with more depreciation taken in early years; therefore, the fraction will have the largest number in the numerator, giving the largest fraction. In the above example, the number for year 1 will be 5, giving 5/15 for the fraction. For the denominator, there is a formula for computing the number:

$$\frac{N\,(N+1)}{2} \quad \text{where } N = \text{number of years of useful life}$$

▲ **Let's use the same asset as was used for straight-line depreciation.** The depreciable base is $105,000.

Year 1	$105,000 X 5/15 = $35,000
Year 2	$105,000 X 4/15 = $28,000
Year 3	$105,000 X 3/15 = $21,000
Year 4	$105,000 X 2/15 = $14,000
Year 5	$105,000 X 1/15 = $ 7,000

Total depreciation taken is $105,000, leaving the book value at $5,000 when the asset is fully depreciated. The total results are the same as for straight-line; the timing is the difference between the two methods.

Note that the **difference between each set of 2 years for sum-of-the-years'-digits is $7,000.** The difference between each fraction is 1/15, and as you can see, $105,000 X 1/15 = $7,000. Knowing that the difference between years must be the same number is a good check for reasonableness when computing depreciation using this method.

▲ **Declining-balance methods are also accelerated methods.** The formula to compute double-declining-balance depreciation is:

Book value X Percentage (double the straight-line rate)

Remember that book value is the difference between an asset's cost and the total in the Accumulated Depreciation account. The straight-line rate is computed by dividing 1 or 100% by the number of years of useful life. For a 5-year useful life, 100% ÷ 5 = 20%. Doubling that rate yields 40%. For an 8-year useful life, 100% ÷ 8 = 12.5%. Doubling that rate yields 25%.

For the same asset:

Year 1	$110,000 X 40% =	$44,000
Year 2	$ 66,000 X 40% =	$26,400
Year 3	$ 39,600 X 40% =	$15,840
Year 4	$ 23,760 X 40% =	$ 9,504
Year 5		$ 9,256*

Often, in the last year of an asset being depreciated using double-declining balance, the depreciation taken is simply the number required to give the proper balance in the Accumulated Depreciation account. **For this asset,** the total must be $105,000 so that the final book value will equal the residual value of $5,000. If we had followed the computations out to the end, then year 5 would have been $ 14,256 X 40% = $ 5,702. This would not have yielded the full $105,000 of depreciation for the asset's life. **In the textbook, the opposite problem occurred.** If the computations had been followed, too much depreciation would have been taken for the last year.

▲ Note that, once again, **the total depreciation taken is $105,000, the same amount taken for the other two methods.** The difference is the timing at which dollar amounts are taken. Note that double-declining-balance yields the highest depreciation for the first year of the asset's life. This method is rather different because residual value is ignored for the initial computations, whereas the other two methods start with the depreciable base.

▲ **Tax laws require the use of the Modified Accelerated Cost Recovery System (MACRS),** which specifies the useful lives to be assigned to different types of assets, as well as the depreciation method to be used.

4. List the factors affecting managers' selection of depreciation methods.

▲ In their **desire to provide financial statement readers with useful information,** managers will select a depreciation method that best reflects the pattern of benefit usage.

▲ **Economic issues may influence a manager's decision,** particularly if a manager's bonus is tied to earnings. In this case, a manager might be motivated to choose a method which results in low depreciation charges and, therefore, high net income. If a loan agreement specifies that certain ratios stay below certain levels, a manager might be motivated to choose a method which will help to effect that.

▲ **Depreciation has nothing to do with valuation of assets.** It simply shows that an asset is being used up and does not attempt to reflect current market value.

▲ **Depreciation has nothing to do with cash flow.** Again, it simply allocates the cost of an asset to expense as the asset is used.

5. Determine which postacquisition expenditures should be expensed and which should be capitalized.

▲ **Expenditures which simply maintain an asset at its current operating level are expensed immediately.** Examples are ordinary, routine maintenance and repairs.

▲ **Expenditures which extend an asset's life or make it more efficient and productive are capitalized.** Examples are an overhaul of an engine or motor and modifications to a machine to make it more efficient.

6. Explain the accounting issues associated with asset write-downs and disposals.

▲ When a **firm disposes of an asset,** cash received is compared with the asset's book value to determine if there is a gain or a loss. Suppose that an asset has a cost of $5,000 and Accumulated Depreciation of $3,000, giving it a book value of $2,000. If the firm sells that asset for $2,300, then there is a gain of $300. On the other hand, if the firm sells that asset for $1,500, then there is a loss of $500. Gains, which increase Retained Earnings, and losses, which reduce Retained Earnings, appear on the income statement.

▲ **When a fixed asset's utility drops below its book value, the asset should be written down so that a firm does not overstate its assets' values.** Write-downs of fixed assets often occur when firms restructure their operations. The

Loss on Writedown reduces Retained Earnings, while the asset is reduced by a like amount. Analysts view write-downs as conservative and generally approve when a company performs them.

7. Interpret financial statement disclosures about noncurrent assets.

▲ **Most balance sheets show one line item for property, plant, and equipment, showing cost less accumulated depreciation.** More detailed disclosures appear in the notes.

▲ **Utilization of fixed assets is measured by the fixed asset turnover ratio.** It is computed by dividing average PPE (net) into net sales. Remember that average PPE is computed by adding the beginning and the ending PPE balances and dividing that sum by 2. Fixed asset turnover reflects the number of sales dollars generated by a $1 investment in PPE. Use of particular depreciation methods, price changes, and the maturity of a firm can all affect the results of this ratio.

▲ **Another ratio is the percentage of PPE depreciated.** This ratio is computed by dividing gross PPE into accumulated depreciation. It permits assessment of the relative age of a firm's assets. Gross PPE is the assets' historical cost.

▲ **The financial statements of U.S. companies do not disclose the market value of fixed assets,** but a few countries do permit the use of market value.

1. Identify three major types of noncurrent assets: (1) property, plant, and equipment, (2) intangible assets, and (3) natural resources. **THIS SECTION WILL DISCUSS INTANGIBLE ASSETS.**

▲ Intangible assets are **long-lived rights.**

▲ **Patents** are granted by the federal government and give the exclusive right to use a product or process for 17 years. Patents protect invention.

▲ **Copyrights** are granted by the federal government and give the exclusive right to use artistic or literary works for a period of 75 years (but a copyright's economic life may be much shorter than its legal life). Copyrights protect artistic and literary works, as opposed to invention.

▲ **Trademarks** are symbols, words, or other distinctive elements used to identify a firm's products. Examples are the Pillsbury Doughboy, McDonald's golden arches and Ronald McDonald, and the Michelin tire man. Trademarks, granted by the federal government, have unlimited legal lives (but their economic lives may be limited).

▲ **Franchises and licenses** are rights to market a particular product or service or to engage in a particular activity. Examples include most of the fast-food restaurants.

▲ **Goodwill** is the difference between the purchase price of a company and the fair value of the identifiable net assets. Goodwill can only arise when one company buys another company. The higher purchase price can be attributed to items such as excellent employees and managers, good training programs, good labor relations, and a valuable customer base.

2. Explain how to account for the acquisition of these assets. **THIS SECTION WILL DISCUSS INTANGIBLE ASSETS.**

▲ **Intangible assets acquired from others** are initially recorded at their historical cost.

▲ **Research and development costs** must be expensed immediately, according to GAAP. If a company buys a patent from another company, then it is allowed to capitalize the entire cost of the patent. If the company, however, develops the patent internally, then all research and development costs are expensed. The only amounts capitalized will be patent filing costs and similar costs. For **computer software costs**, costs are expensed until technological feasibility is demonstrated. Thereafter, costs are capitalized.

3. Describe the procedures for depreciation, amortization, and depletion. **THIS SECTION WILL DISCUSS AMORTIZATION.**

▲ The **costs of intangible assets must be allocated to expense over their lives.** Instead of calling this process "depreciation," for intangible assets, the process is called "amortization." Amortization is computed on a straight-line basis, and the maximum amortization period is 40 years.

▲ **When amortization is recorded,** Amortization Expense, which reduces Retained Earnings, is increased, and the intangible asset itself is decreased. **No contra-asset account is used,** different from the procedure for fixed assets for which Accumulated Depreciation is used. If a company paid $30,000 for a patent which it estimates will have a useful life of 5 years, then it will record $6,000 amortization expense a year for the 5 years ($30,000 ÷ 5 years).

1. Identify three major types of noncurrent assets: (1) property, plant, and equipment, (2) intangible assets, and (3) natural resources. **THIS SECTION WILL DISCUSS NATURAL RESOURCES.**

▲ **Natural resources** are assets such as mines, wells, and timberlands. These assets are also called wasting assets.

2. Explain how to account for the acquisition of these assets. **THIS SECTION WILL DISCUSS NATURAL RESOURCES.**

▲ **Natural resources acquired from others are valued at their historical cost.** A firm, however, may self-explore and develop sites. If a firm does this, then GAAP permits two methods to account for the costs of exploration. **The full cost method** capitalizes as an asset the exploration costs of both successful and unsuccessful sites. **The successful efforts method** expenses immediately the cost of unsuccessful sites: Only costs of developing successful sites are capitalized.

3. Describe the procedures for depreciation, amortization, and depletion. **THIS SECTION WILL DISCUSS DEPLETION.**

▲ As is true for fixed and intangible assets, **the costs of natural resources must be allocated to expense as the natural resources are consumed.** This process is called depletion.

▲ **To compute depletion expense per unit**, the following formula is used:

(Historical cost - Residual value) ÷ Estimated units

Once a unit cost is computed, that cost is multiplied by the number of units extracted and sold during the accounting period. For example, a company purchased timberland for $1,000,000, estimating the residual value at $100,000 and the number of board feet of timber at 1,800,000. Depletion expense per board foot is $ .50 ($1,000,000 - $100,000) ÷ 1,800,000 board feet. If 300,000 board feet are harvested and sold, then depletion expense will be $150,000 (300,000 X $ .50). Depletion expense, which reduces Retained Earnings, is increased, as is a contra-asset account, Accumulated Depletion.

CHAPTER SELF-TEST

Note: The notation (CO1) means that the question was drawn from chapter objective number one.

Matching

Please write the letters of the following terms in the spaces to the left of the definitions.

a. Amortization
b. Book value
c. Declining-balance method
d. Depletion
e. Depreciable base
f. Depreciation
g. Residual value
h. Sum-of-the-years'-digits method

_____ 1. (CO3) Cost less salvage value.

_____ 2. (CO3) Process which shows that a natural resource is being used up or consumed.

_____ 3. (CO3) Amount for which a company expects to sell an asset after it is finished using it.

_____ 4. (CO3) Cost less accumulated depreciation.

_____ 5. (CO3) Process which allocates the cost of an intangible asset to expense.

_____ 6. (CO3) Depreciation method which multiplies the book value of an asset by a percentage.

_____ 7. (CO3) Process which allocates the cost of a property, plant, and equipment asset to expense.

_____ 8. (CO3) Depreciation method which multiplies the depreciable base of an asset by a fraction.

Completion

Please write in the word or words which will complete the sentence.

1. (CO2) Fixed assets are initially valued at their _________________________ _________________________.

2. (CO3) Depreciation is recorded during each accounting period in order to apply the ___________________ principle.

3. (CO3) An asset has a cost of $9,000, accumulated depreciation of $3,000, and a residual value of $1,000. The depreciable base of the asset is ______________.

4. (CO3) If an asset has an estimated useful life of 9 years and the sum-of-the-years'-digits method of depreciation is used, then the denominator of the fraction is ______________.

5. (CO3) The double-declining-balance and sum-of-the-years'-digits methods of depreciation are examples of ______________ depreciation methods.

6. (CO5) If a company performs routine maintenance on a fixed asset, the proper accounting for the expenditure is to ______________ it immediately.

7. (CO1) Long-lived assets which convey legal rights are called ______________ assets.

8. (CO1) ______________ is the excess of the purchase price of a business over the fair value of its identifiable net assets.

9. (CO2) GAAP require that research and development costs be ______________ immediately.

10. (CO2) With respect to natural resources, the ______________ ______________ method capitalizes as an asset the exploration costs of both successful and unsuccessful sites.

Multiple Choice

Please circle the correct answer.

1. (CO2) A company purchased a machine for $50,000. Because it paid within 10 days, the company was granted a $1,000 discount. Sales taxes totaled $3,000, shipping charges were $500, and installation charges were $250. The total cost capitalized to the Machinery account is:
   a. $53,750.
   b. $52,750.
   c. $52,500.
   d. $52,250.

2. (CO3) A piece of equipment cost $10,000, has a residual value of $1,000, and an estimated useful life of 5 years. The company uses straight-line depreciation. What is the equipment's book value at the end of the second year?
   a. $1,800.
   b. $3,600.
   c. $5,400.
   d. $6,400.

3. (CO3) A machine cost $5,000, has a salvage value of $500, and has an estimated useful life of 8 years. The company uses double-declining-balance depreciation. What is depreciation expense for the second year?
   a. $1,250.00.
   b. $1,125.00.
   c. $ 937.50.
   d. $ 843.75.

4. (CO3) Which of the following methods gives the highest total depreciation expense for an asset?
   a. Straight-line.
   b. Sum-of-the-years'-digits.
   c. Double-declining-balance.
   d. All of the above give the same total amount of depreciation expense.

5. (CO6) A company owns a machine with a cost of $6,000, a residual value of $400, and accumulated depreciation of $2,100. It has contracted to sell the machine for $4,100. The company will, therefore, have a:
   a. gain of $200.
   b. loss of $200.
   c. gain of $1,500.
   d. loss of $1,500.

6. (CO7) A firm has net sales for the year of $5,000,000. The beginning net PPE is $2,000,000, while the ending balance of net PPE is $3,000,000. What is the fixed asset turnover?
   a. 2.50.
   b. 2.00.
   c. 1.67.
   d. .50.

7. (CO2) With respect to natural resources, which method expenses immediately the cost of unsuccessful sites?
   a. Straight-line method.
   b. Full cost method.
   c. Successful efforts method.
   d. Declining-balance method.

8. (CO1) Which of the following intangible assets protects the creators of artistic and literary works?
   a. Copyright.
   b. Patent.
   c. Trademark.
   d. License.

9. (CO3) A firm purchased a patent for $10,000 and estimates that the patent will have a useful life of 5 years. When the firm amortizes the patent, it will:
   a. increase Retained Earnings and decrease Patent for $2,000.
   b. increase Amortization Expense and increase Accumulated Amortization for $2,000.
   c. decrease Amortization Expense and decrease Accumulated Amortization for $2,000.
   d. increase Amortization Expense and decrease Patent for $2,000.

10. (CO3) A company purchased a mineral mine for $1,500,000. It estimates that the salvage of the land after the mine is depleted is $300,000 and that 2,400,000 ounces of minerals can be mined. In the first year of production, the company mines and sells 500,000 ounces. What is depletion expense for the year?
   a. $1,000,000.
   b. $ 800,000.
   c. $ 312,500.
   d. $ 250,000.

<u>Demonstration Problem</u>

Spinnaker Corporation purchased a piece of machinery on January 3, 1996, for $48,000. The corporation estimates that the residual value will be $6,000 and that the estimated useful life of the machine will be 6 years.

REQUIRED:

1. Please compute depreciation expense for 1996 - 1998 using straight-line depreciation.

2. Please compute depreciation expense for 1996 - 1998 using sum-of-the-years'-digits.

3. Please compute depreciation expense for 1996 - 1998 using double-declining-balance.

4. Consider your answers in number 1 above. If the machine is sold in early 1999 for $30,000, then what is the gain or loss on the sale? On what financial statement do gains and losses appear? How will the company record the sale?

SOLUTIONS TO SELF-TEST

Matching

1. e
2. d
3. g
4. b
5. a
6. c
7. f
8. h

Completion

1. historical cost
2. matching
3. $8,000
4. 45
5. accelerated
6. expense
7. intangible
8. Goodwill
9. expensed
10. full cost

Multiple Choice

1. b
2. d
3. c
4. d
5. a
6. b
7. c
8. a
9. d
10. d

Demonstration Problem

1. $48,000 - $6,000 = $42,000 depreciable base ÷ 6 years = $7,000 per year

2. Sum-of-the-years'-digits = 21 (6 + 5 + 4 + 3 + 2 + 1)

1996	$42,000 X 6/21 = $12,000
1997	$42,000 X 5/21 = $10,000
1998	$42,000 X 4/21 = $ 8,000

3. 100% ÷ 6 = .166666 X 2 = .33333 or 1/3

1996	\$48,000 X 1/3 =	\$16,000
1997	\$32,000 X 1/3 =	\$10,667 (rounded)
1998	\$21,333 X 1/3 =	\$ 7,111

Note that straight-line and sum-of-the-years'-digits both start with the depreciable base, while double-declining-balance starts with the book value, which in the first year is the cost of the asset.

4. There will be a gain of \$3,000. The book value at the end of 1998 is \$27,000 (\$48,000 - \$21,000 accumulated depreciation). Since \$30,000 is received, the extra \$3,000 is a gain. Both gains and losses appear on a firm's income statement. The company will do the following to record the sale: decrease the asset by \$48,000, decrease Accumulated Depreciation by \$21,000, increase Cash by \$30,000, and increase Gain on Disposal by \$3,000.

CHAPTER 8

CURRENT LIABILITIES

CHAPTER OVERVIEW

Chapter 8 examines the current liabilities section of the balance sheet. You will learn about the various types of current liabilities reported on the balance sheets of most business firms. You will learn about how some liabilities have a definite payment amount while others are based on estimates and judgments. The appendix to the chapter examines the time value of money and shows you how to use tables to compute the future amount and the present value of single sums as well as of annuities.

Review of Specific Chapter Objectives

1. Recognize the types of current liabilities that are reported on the balance sheets of most business firms.
2. Understand the types of business transactions and events that create current liabilities.
3. Appreciate how liability reporting often depends on estimates and judgments.

- ▲ **Current liabilities** are short-term obligations that usually must be paid from current assets within a year. There are **three types:** 1) obligations to pay cash to another entity, 2) obligations to provide goods or services to another entity, and 3) obligations to honor product warranties.

- ▲ The following sections will discuss **liabilities requiring cash payments.**

- ▲ **Accounts payable** represent debts that the firm incurs in purchasing inventories and supplies, as well as amounts that the firm owes for other services used in its operations. **Suppliers often offer discounts to induce early payment.** If a company purchases $5,000 of supplies with terms of 2/10, n/30 and intends to pay within the discount period, then it generally records the purchase at the net price (in this case, $4,900). If the company fails to pay within the discount period and must remit the full $5,000, then the $100 discount not taken becomes interest expense.

▲ **Notes payable** are more formal promises to pay a lender. They are usually in writing and involve payment of interest. Notes may be **interestbearing**. When a borrower goes to a bank to borrow $50,000, he is given the entire $50,000. At the maturity date, he must repay not only the principal of $50,000 but also interest. Notes may also be **discounted**. A firm signs a note, with an interest rate of 10%, promising to repay $50,000 in six months, but receives only $47,500. The bank has deducted the interest ($50,000 X .10 X 6/12) at the time of the borrowing. Despite the receipt of $47,500, the company must repay $50,000 at the maturity date. At that time the company will recognize interest expense of $2,500.

▲ **Accrued liabilities** represent expenses that have been incurred prior to the balance sheet date which have been neither paid nor included with liabilities as of the balance sheet date. An adjustment, increasing both an expense and a liability, must be made at the balance sheet date. For many companies, these accrued liabilities include accrued wages and salaries and accrued vacation and sick pay.

▲ **Long-term debts often have a current portion or become current as time goes by.** An example of the former is a 30-year mortgage. Remember that each mortgage payment consists of both principal and interest. On the balance sheet date, the principal component of the next 12 payments must be classified as a current liability. An example of the latter is a 5-year note payable, a long-term liability. Twelve months before the maturity date, the entire note must be classified as a current liability.

▲ **Accrued income taxes** are certainly a current liability because they are due within one year and generally sooner than that.

▲ **Restructuring costs** occur when a company decides to downsize and to refocus its operations. When a firm decides to restructure, the total estimated costs of restructuring are expensed in the current year. This involves increasing both an expense and a liability.

▲ As noted above, a company may also have **obligations to provide goods or services**. A magazine publisher is a good example. When a person subscribes to take the magazine for one year, the company receives the entire year's subscription amount in advance. The Cash account is increased, as is a liability account called Advance Payments from Customers. The liability represents the company's obligation to provide the subscriber not with money but with a magazine each month over the next twelve months. As each magazine is sent, the company reduces its liability and finally recognizes revenue.

▲ The third type of liability is an **obligation to honor product warranties.** Companies usually stand behind the quality of the products they sell and offer to repair defective products or to refund the purchase price. The matching principle dictates that these possible costs must be matched with current sales revenues. The future costs must be estimated and recorded in the period of the sale. This will involve an increase in both Warranty Expense and Warranty Obligation. Estimates are derived from the company's past experience and from industry averages.

Review of Specific Appendix Objectives

1. Determine the future value, or compound amount, of dollars that are invested or borrowed today.
2. Determine the value today, or present value, of dollars that are to be received or paid in the future.
3. Understand how the concept of present value is used to calculate interest expense.

▲ **Money deposited in a bank account will grow larger because it earns interest.** Simple interest is interest ONLY on the principal. If you deposit $1,000 in a bank account and it earns simple interest of 8% per year, then you will earn $80 of interest each year. Compound interest, however, is interest that is paid both on principal and on interest. If you deposit $1,000 in a bank account and it earns 8% interest compounded each year, then you will earn $80 of interest in year one. In year two, however, interest will be computed on $1,080, the sum of the original principal and the first year's interest.

▲ It is **often necessary in business settings to compute the future value and the present value of sums of money.** Only if a transaction involves the short-term (less than one year) can future and present values be ignored. **Present value** is the term used to denote the value today of cash to be received or paid in future periods. **Future value** is the term used to denote the expected maturity value of cash that is deposited or invested today at a specified rate of interest for a given number of future periods.

▲ There is a formula for the **future value of a single sum,** but most often, accountants and businesspeople use tables, financial calculators, or electronic spreadsheets for the computations. The future value table allows the accountant to answer the following type of question: If I deposit a certain amount of money in the bank at a certain interest rate for a certain length of time, then how much will I have in the account at a future date?

▲ Business decisions often require that the accountant **determine the value today, or present value, of a single amount to be received or paid in the future.** Again, while there is a formula for this, tables, financial calculators, or electronic spreadsheets are usually used for the computations. The present value table allows the accountant to answer the following type of question: If I need a certain amount of money available in the future, then how much do I need to deposit in the bank now at a certain interest rate for a certain period of time to make sure that I will have that amount of money? When interest rates are used to compute present values instead of future amounts, the interest rate is usually referred to as the discount rate.

▲ Certainly the **choice of an interest or discount rate requires great judgment.** The rate chosen will have a large effect on the outcome of the calculations. Rates chosen by lenders and investors vary directly with risk.

▲ In addition to performing computations involving single sums of money, there are also **computations involving annuities.** The term annuity describes equal cash flows over uniform time intervals. Notice that the cash flow can be either an inflow or an outflow. Again, tables can be used for computations, as can financial calculators and electronic spreadsheets.

▲ To determine the **present value of an annuity,** tables can be used. The present value of an annuity table allows the accountant to answer the following type of question: What is the value today of a series of payments I will receive or make in the future? The present value factors for annuities are equal to the sum of the present value factors for the individual cash flows.

▲ To determine the **future value of an annuity,** tables can be used. The future value of an annuity table allows the accountant to answer the following type of question: What is the future value of a series of payments I will make or receive over several periods of time? A common example of the need for this type of computation is a sinking fund, a fund set up by a firm for a designated purpose, such as the retirement of outstanding debt or the replacement of operating assets.

▲ In performing present and future value computations, there are basically **two questions that you need to ask:**
1. Do I need to know the present value or the future value?
2. Is the money a single amount or a series of payments (and, thus, an annuity)?

It is easy to become confounded when working with the tables. Make sure that you ask yourself the two questions, and make sure that you use the correct table.

CHAPTER SELF-TEST

Note: The notation (CO1) means that the question was drawn from chapter objective number one.

Matching

Please write the letters of the following terms in the spaces to the left of the definitions.

a. Accounts payable
b. Accrued liabilities
c. Future value
d. Note payable
e. Present value
f. Restructuring
g. Warranty

_____ 1. (CO) Formal written promise, usually involving interest, to repay a sum of money at a specified time in the future.

_____ 2. (CO) Company's promise to stand behind the quality of its products.

_____ 3. (CO) A firm's downsizing and refocusing of its operations.

_____ 4. (CO) Debts incurred by a firm in purchasing inventories and supplies, as well as amounts that it owes for services used in its operations.

_____ 5. (App) Dollar amount to which a sum of money invested today will grow.

_____ 6. (CO) Expenses incurred prior to the balance sheet date that have been neither paid nor included with liabilities as of the balance sheet date.

_____ 7. (App) Value today of a sum of money that will be paid or received in the future.

Completion

Please write in the word or words which will complete the sentence.

1. (App) When interest rates are used to compute present values, the interest rate is usually referred to as the ____________________ rate.

2. (CO) ____________________ liabilities are short-term obligations that usually must be paid from current assets within a year.

3. (App) The term ____________________ is used to describe equal cash flows over uniform time intervals.

4. (CO) If a firm signs a note for $10,000, promising to repay $10,300 at the maturity date, then the firm has signed a ____________________ note, in which the bank has deducted the ____________________ in advance.

5. (App) If a company knows that it must invest $3,000 today in order to have that amount grow to $5,000 by a future date, then the $3,000 is called the ____________________ value.

6. (CO) A concert promoter receives $75 for a ticket to a concert he will provide in six months: He increases both Cash and a liability account. When he provides the concert, then he will ____________________ the liability and ____________________ a revenue account.

7. (App) The concept of earning interest on interest is called ____________________ interest.

8. (App) A fund, the ending balance of which is usually designated for a special purpose, is called a ____________________ fund.

Multiple Choice

Please circle the correct answer.

1. (CO) Which of the following is an example of a current liability?
   a. Obligation to pay cash to another entity.
   b. Obligation to provide other entities with goods or services for which payment has already been received.
   c. Obligation to honor product warranties.
   d. All of the above are examples of current liabilities.

2. (CO) A company purchased supplies on account. When the company pays the bill, it will:
   a. increase Supplies and decrease Cash.
   b. increase Accounts Payable and decrease Cash.
   c. decrease Accounts Payable and decrease Cash.
   d. decrease Accounts Payable and decrease Supplies.

3. (CO) A company purchased inventory costing $2,000 on account and intends to take advantage of the 2/10, n/30 discount terms. It, therefore, recorded the purchase at the net amount of $1,960. Unfortunately, it did not pay within the discount period. To record the payment transaction, the company will:
   a. decrease both Cash and Accounts Payable by $2,000.
   b. decrease Cash by $2,000, decrease Accounts Payable by $1,960, and increase Interest Expense by $40.
   c. decrease both Cash and Accounts Payable by $1,960.
   d. decrease Cash by $1,960, decrease Accounts Payable by $1,960, and increase Interest Expense by $40.

4. (CO) A company's vacation pay and sick pay are examples of:
   a. accrued liabilities.
   b. warranties.
   c. accounts payable.
   d. current maturities of long-term debt.

5. (CO) At December 31, 1998, a firm has a mortgage payable of $10,000. Principal payments due within the next year total $1,200. How will the firm report the liability on the balance sheet dated December 31, 1998?
   a. Long-term liabilities, $10,000; current liabilities, $1,200.
   b. Only long-term liabilities, $10,000.
   c. Only current liabilities, $1,200.
   d. Long-term liabilities, $8,800; current liabilities, $1,200.

6. (CO) When a firm decides to restructure, in recording the restructuring, it will typically:
   a. increase both Retained Earnings and a liability account.
   b. decrease both Retained Earnings and a liability account.
   c. increase both an expense and a liability account.
   d. increase both asset accounts and a liability account.

7. (CO) A magazine publisher receives $48 for a year's subscription to its magazine. One month later, it sends out the first magazine. When the cash is received, the liability account is ____________; when the magazine is sent out, the liability is ____________.
   a. increased; decreased.
   b. decreased; increased.
   c. increased; increased.
   d. decreased; decreased.

8. (App) A customer deposited $500 in a bank at an interest rate of 6%. No more deposits were made in the first two years, and the balance in the account at the end of the second year was $560. The depositor has earned:
   a. compound interest.
   b. simple interest.
   c. partial interest.
   d. discounted interest.

9. (App) A customer deposited $500 in a bank at an interest rate of 6%. No more deposits were made in the first two years, and the balance in the account at the end of the second year was $561.80. The depositor has earned:
   a. compound interest.
   b. simple interest.
   c. partial interest.
   d. discounted interest.

10. (App) Which of the following statements is true?
   a. The value today of an amount to be received or paid in the future is called the future value.
   b. The term annualization is used to describe equal cash flows over uniform time intervals.
   c. Present value is the term used to denote the expected maturity value of cash that is deposited today at a specified rate of interest for a given number of future periods.
   d. The value today of an amount to be received or paid in the future is called the present value.

Demonstration Problems

1. You must pay your sister $3,000 in five years. How much money must you deposit today in a bank account, earning 6% interest per year, in order to be able to pay her that sum? Use the factors given.

Future Value of $1	5 periods, 6%	1.338
Future Value of an Annuity	5 periods, 6%	5.637
Present Value of $1	5 periods, 6%	0.747
Present Value of an Annuity	5 periods, 6%	4.212

2. You have just received $5,000 in checks for your college graduation present and have decided to deposit them in the bank. How much will you have in the account at the end of five years, assuming that it will earn 6% interest per year? Use the factors given.

Future Value of $1	5 periods, 6%	1.338
Future Value of an Annuity	5 periods, 6%	5.637
Present Value of $1	5 periods, 6%	0.747
Present Value of an Annuity	5 periods, 6%	4.212

3. You have decided to set up an investment account for yourself and will deposit $1,000 in the account at the end of every year for five years. Assuming that the account will earn 6% interest per year, how much will you have in the account at the end of five years? Use the factors given.

Future Value of $1	5 periods, 6%	1.338
Future Value of an Annuity	5 periods, 6%	5.637
Present Value of $1	5 periods, 6%	0.747
Present Value of an Annuity	5 periods, 6%	4.212

SOLUTIONS TO SELF-TEST

Matching

1. d
2. g
3. f
4. a
5. c
6. b
7. e

Completion

1. discount
2. Current
3. annuity
4. discounted, interest
5. present
6. reduce, increase
7. compound
8. sinking

Multiple Choice

1. d
2. c
3. b
4. a
5. d
6. c
7. a
8. b
9. a
10. d

Demonstration Problems

1. $3,000 X 0.747 = $2,241

2. $5,000 X 1.338 = $6,690

3. $1,000 X 5.637 = $5,637

CHAPTER 9

NONCURRENT LIABILITIES

CHAPTER OVERVIEW

Chapter 9 examines a variety of noncurrent liabilities. You will learn about notes and bonds, including bonds sold at an amount other than par value. You will also learn about interest computations for both notes and bonds. Features such as restrictive covenants, collateral, and convertibility will be discussed, as will purchase commitments and contingent liabilities. You will learn about the reasons for deferred taxes and how to account for deferred tax liabilities and deferred tax assets.

Review of Specific Chapter Objectives

1. Recognize the types of noncurrent obligations that are reported by business firms.

   ▲ **Noncurrent liabilities** represent obligations of the firm that generally are due more than one year after the balance sheet date. The major portion of these liabilities consists of **notes payable and bonds payable.**

2. Comprehend features of long-term borrowing contracts, i.e., notes and bonds payable.
3. Determine periodic interest expense and the valuation of noncurrent obligations in financial reports.

   ▲ **Long-term notes payable can be either interest-bearing or discounted.** With an interest-bearing note, the bank will loan the principal of the note for a specified period. The borrower will pay interest periodically and will repay the principal at the maturity date. Interest expense, of course, reduces Retained Earnings, as do all expenses.

▲ **Discounted notes** do not require periodic payments of interest. If a company borrows $50,000 for 3 years and, because of the terms of the note, will not make periodic interest payments, then the lender will be unwilling to provide the borrower the full $50,000 face amount of the note. **All long-term financing agreements involve interest, regardless of whether it is separately identified.** In this case, the note must be discounted, and the lender will lend the present value of the note, as computed by using the compound interest tables. Assuming an interest rate of 8%, a factor of 0.794 is pulled from the Present Value of $1 table at 3n and 8%. Multiplying $50,000 by the factor, the present value (the amount which the borrower will receive in cash) is computed as $39,700. The difference, $10,300, is the discount, which represents the interest that is associated with the transaction. It will be recognized as Interest Expense by the borrower over the 3-year period of the note. At the maturity date, the borrower will repay $50,000 to the lender.

▲ **Bonds payable represent a major source of borrowed capital for U.S. companies.** Bonds are individual notes, sold to individual investors as well as to financial institutions. They have several advantages: 1) The sale of bonds provides access to a large pool of lenders; 2) for some firms, selling bonds may be less expensive than other forms of borrowing; and 3) bond financing may offer managers greater flexibility in the future.

▲ **Bonds involve the periodic payment of interest (usually every six months) and the repayment of the principal amount.** The predicted interest rate usually becomes the coupon or face or nominal rate: It sets the cash interest payments the company will have to make. If the principal of a bond is $500,000 and the coupon rate is 6%, then the company will pay $30,000 ($500,000 X 6%) cash interest each year, or $15,000 every six months. The market rate of interest will be known only when the bonds are sold. Because interest rates change constantly, it is rare that a bond coupon rate will equal the market rate when the bond is sold.

▲ **Bonds sell at par or face value when the coupon rate equals the market rate of interest on the date of sale.** For the bond noted above, on the date of sale, both Cash and Bonds Payable will increase by $500,000. On each of the two annual interest payment dates, Interest Expense will increase and Cash will decrease by $15,000. On the maturity date, both Cash and Bonds Payable will decrease by $500,000.

▲ **When interest is paid each six months, the interest rate is said to be compounded semiannually.** If, on the date of sale, the coupon rate does not equal the market rate, the bonds will sell at their present value. Note this about the present value computations: Since the bonds pay interest twice a year, the interest rate must be halved (10% per year is 5% each six months) and the number of years must be doubled (a 6-year bond pays interest 12 times over the life of the bond).

▲ **If the coupon rate is below the market rate of interest on the date of sale, then the bonds will sell at a discount.** An investor will not pay face amount for a bond which has an interest rate lower than that which the investor could find elsewhere.

▲ The following is an **example of a bond sold at a discount.** On January 3 a company sells $2,000,000 of bonds with a coupon rate of interest of 9% while the market rate of interest is 10%. The bonds are 10-year bonds and pay interest each June 30 and December 31. The present value of the bonds is:

$2,000,000 X 0.377	=	$ 754,000	(Present Value of $1)
$ 90,000 X 12.462	=	1,121,580	(Present Value of Ann.)
		$1,875,580	

Please note the following important points:

1. The coupon rate of interest is used to compute the cash interest payments ($2,000,000 X .09 X 6/12) and to compare against the market rate of interest (9% versus 10%) to let you know that the bonds are selling at a discount. After that, the present value computations and interest computations are driven by the market rate of interest.
2. Because the bonds are 10-year bonds paying interest twice a year, there are 20 interest payment periods, and the market rate of interest will be halved, to 5%. Both factors are from the 20n, 5% columns of the appropriate tables.

▲ Upon sale of the bonds, the company will **increase Cash and net Bonds Payable by $1,875,580.** The discount of $124,420 represents additional interest paid to bondholders. When periodic interest expense differs from the periodic cash payments to the bondholders, the reported value of the bonds will be adjusted for the difference through a process called amortization. For our bond, the first interest payment date will involve the following: a decrease in Cash of $90,000, an increase in Interest Expense of $93,379 ($1,875,580 X 5%), and an increase in the reported value of Bonds Payable (because the discount is decreasing) of $3,379 ($93,379 - $90,000). The value of the bonds will continue to rise toward $2,000,000 over the life of the bond, and the discount will be completely amortized by the maturity date.

▲ The following is an example of a **bond sold at a premium:** This occurs because the coupon rate of interest is higher than the market rate. We'll use the same bond as was used above in the discount situation: On January 3 a company sells $2,000,000 of bonds with a coupon rate of interest of 9%, but now the market rate of interest is 8%. The bonds are 10-year bonds and pay interest each June 30 and December 31. The present value of the bonds is:

$2,000,000 X 0.456 =	$ 912,000	(Present Value of $1)
$ 90,000 X 13.590 =	1,223,100	(Present Value of Ann.)
	$2,135,100	

The factors are pulled from the 20n, 4% columns of the appropriate tables.

▲ Upon sale of the bonds, the company will **increase Cash and total Bonds Payable by $2,135,100.** The premium of $135,100 represents a reduction in interest paid to bondholders to compensate for the fact that the coupon rate is too high. Just as was true for bonds sold at a discount, the reported value of the bonds will be adjusted for the difference between interest expense and cash interest payments through a process called amortization. For our bond, the first interest payment date will involve the following: a decrease in Cash of $90,000, an increase in Interest Expense of $85,404 ($2,135,100 X 4%), and a decrease in the reported value of Bonds Payable (because the premium is decreasing) of $4,596 ($90,000 - $85,404). The value of the bonds will continue to fall toward $2,000,000 over the life of the bond, and the premium will be completely amortized by the maturity date.

▲ **Changes in market rates of interest may motivate firms to buy back their outstanding bonds prior to their scheduled maturity dates.** Any difference between the reported value of the bonds and the repurchase price must be accounted for as either an extraordinary gain or loss. Extraordinary gains or losses are reported separately, net of tax, at the bottom of the income statement.

▲ **A lender may insist that a borrower agree to various restrictions in order that the lender be protected from possible default by the borrower.** Violations of these restrictive covenants constitute technical default on the debt and usually come with penalties for the borrower. Analysts are always concerned with the existence of such covenants.

- ▲ **Debt agreements sometimes require that specific assets of the borrower be pledged as security in the event of default by the borrower.** If a lender is not happy with the assets to be pledged as collateral, then he may require that a sinking fund be established to secure the debt. Such a fund is segregated cash and/or investments, administered by a third party, dedicated to repayment of the debt.

- ▲ Sometimes **bonds are convertible**, meaning that the bondholder has the option to exchange the debt for a predetermined number of shares of stock. Investors usually view convertibility as a very attractive feature. Issuing companies often add the convertibility feature to make the issue more attractive without having to offer a higher rate of interest on the bonds.

4. Be alert to additional business obligations that presently are unreported.

- ▲ **Commitments** are agreements with suppliers, customers, employers, or other entities that are not yet completed transactions and consequently have not been recognized in the accounts. Commitments are often transacted so that a buyer may lock in what seems to be a favorable price. If significant, then these commitments should be disclosed in the notes to the financial statements.

- ▲ **Contingencies** are existing conditions whose resulting gains and losses are presently uncertain but will be resolved by the occurrence of future events. As is true for commitments, **contingencies are classified as either current or noncurrent liabilities, or they may only be disclosed in the notes.**

5. Appreciate why income is measured differently for income tax and financial reporting purposes.

- ▲ **Income measures for financial reporting purposes** should help financial analysts to assess the firm's future ability to generate cash. **Income measures for income tax purposes** must comply with the relevant provisions of the IRS tax code.

6. Understand why the tax basis and the financial reporting basis of assets and liabilities may differ.
7. Interpret financial statement measurements of income tax expense and deferred income tax liability.

- ▲ **Book measurements** are used for financial reporting purposes, while **tax measurements** must comply with income tax laws. In most cases, **differences between book and tax measurements are temporary in nature.**

- ▲ **Accounting standards for reporting income tax expenses and**

liabilities reflect a basic premise: All events that affect the tax impact of temporary differences should be recognized currently in the financial statements. Two types of events can affect these expected tax impacts: a change in the amount of temporary differences between the book and the tax bases of a firm's assets (or liabilities) and a change in tax rates that will apply to those temporary differences.

- **A frequently occurring temporary difference appears in the area of depreciation.** A company may use straight-line depreciation for the books but an accelerated method for tax depreciation. Use of the accelerated method will lower current net, and therefore taxable, income. The temporary difference simply allows a firm to postpone its tax payments to later years: The tax eventually must be paid. Thus, accounting standards require that firms recognize a liability for such future income taxes. **The liability for future income taxes is referred to as a deferred income tax liability.** It is computed by multiplying the difference between the asset's book and tax bases by the appropriate income tax rate. If a company owns assets with a book basis of $7,000,000 and a tax basis of $5,000,000, and if the income tax rate is 40%, then the deferred income tax liability is $800,000 ($7,000,000 - $5,000,000 = $2,000,000 X 40%).

- **Deferred tax accounting appears to provide a better matching of expenses on the income statement, at least when tax rates are expected to be stable over time.**

- **Others items causing temporary differences** include revenue and expense measurements in areas such as leasing, warranties, debt refinancing, and exchanges of assets. Just as there are deferred tax liabilities, there are also **deferred tax assets.** These occur when the difference between book and tax measurements results in earlier recognition of taxable income: The reduction in income tax will occur in future years.

- To sum up, a **deferred tax liability** causes current taxable income to be lower than book income. The increase in tax occurs in future years. A **deferred tax asset** causes current taxable income to be higher than book income. The benefit, the decrease in income tax, will occur in future years.

- **Deferred tax obligations are classified as current or noncurrent based upon the current or noncurrent classification of the related asset.** While long-term obligations are reported at their present values, deferred tax obligations are not discounted to their present values.

CHAPTER SELF-TEST

Note: The notation (CO1) means that the question was drawn from chapter objective number one.

Matching

Please write the letters of the following terms in the spaces to the left of the definitions.

a. Bond
b. Commitments
c. Contingencies
d. Discount on bonds
e. Noninterest-bearing note
f. Par value
g. Restrictive covenants
h. Temporary differences

_____ 1. (CO4) Agreements with suppliers, customers, employers, or other entities that are not yet completed transactions and have not been recognized in the accounts.

_____ 2. (CO2,3) Individual notes, sold to individual investors as well as to financial institutions: a major source of borrowed capital for U.S. firms.

_____ 3. (CO2,3) Another name for face value.

_____ 4. (CO2,3) Security which does not entail periodic interest payments and is sold at a discount.

_____ 5. (CO4) Existing conditions whose resulting gains and losses are presently uncertain but will be resolved by the occurrence of future events.

_____ 6. (CO2,3) Occurs when a bond's coupon rate of interest is below the market rate of interest.

_____ 7. (CO6,7) Occur when taxable income differs from financial reporting income.

_____ 8. (CO2,3) Often part of loan contracts; violation constitutes technical default.

Completion

Please write in the word or words which will complete the sentence.

1. (CO2,3) If a bond's coupon rate of interest is higher than the market rate of interest, then the bond will sell at a ________________________.

2. (CO2,3) Both bond premium and discount must be ________________________ so that the reported value of a bond at the maturity date is equal to the face value.

3. (CO2,3) If a company repurchases its bonds, then any difference between the reported value and the repurchase price must be recognized as an ________________________ gain or loss.

4. (CO2,3) If a note is a non-interest-bearing note, then the borrower will receive the ________________ ________________ of the note on the date of the borrowing.

5. (CO1) Liabilities due more than one year after the balance sheet date are ________________________ liabilities.

6. (CO2,3) ________________________ refers to specific assets of the firm which must be pledged as security for debt in the event of default by the borrower.

7. (CO2,3) Bonds which may be exchanged for shares of stock in a company are said to be ________________________.

8. (CO6,7) ________________________ is the cause of most temporary differences for companies.

Multiple Choice

Please circle the correct answer.

1. (CO2,3) If a bond's coupon rate coincides with the market rate of interest when the bonds are sold to investors, then the bonds will sell at:
   a. a premium.
   b. a discount.
   c. par value.
   d. a discounted value.

2. (CO2,3) The interest rate of a bond is 10%, the bond is a 6-year bond, and it pays interest twice a year. The factor from the compound interest tables must be the factor at:
   a. 6n, 10%.
   b. 12n, 5%.
   c. 12n, 10%.
   d. 6n, 5%.

3. (CO6,7) If a company has a deferred tax liability, then in future years the company will:
   a. pay more tax than in the current year.
   b. pay less tax than in the current year.
   c. pay the same tax as in the current year.
   d. None of the above is correct.

4. (CO6,7) To determine the amount of a deferred tax liability:
   a. taxable income is multiplied by the appropriate tax rate.
   b. book income is multiplied by the appropriate tax rate.
   c. the sum of an asset's book and tax bases is multiplied by the appropriate tax rate.
   d. the difference between an asset's book and tax bases is multiplied by the appropriate tax rate.

5. (CO6,7) If a company has a deferred tax asset, then in future years the company will:
   a. pay more tax than in the current year.
   b. pay less tax than in the current year.
   c. pay the same tax as in the current year.
   d. None of the above is correct.

6. (CO6,7) Which of the following statements is correct?
   a. Deferred tax liabilities are classified only as current liabilities.
   b. Deferred tax liabilities are classified only as noncurrent liabilities.
   c. Deferred tax liabilities are considered to be contra-liability accounts.
   d. Deferred tax liabilities are classified based upon the current versus noncurrent classification of the related asset.

7. (CO2,3) Other names for coupon rate of interest are:
   a. face rate and nominal rate.
   b. face rate and market rate.
   c. nominal rate and market rate.
   d. discounted rate and market rate.

8. (CO2,3) If a bond sells at a discount, then:
   a. interest expense is the same as the cash payment for interest.
   b. interest expense is lower than the cash payment for interest.
   c. interest expense is higher than the cash payment for interest.
   d. None of the above is correct.

9. (CO2,3) If a bond sells at a premium, then:
   a. interest expense is the same as the cash payment for interest.
   b. interest expense is lower than the cash payment for interest.
   c. interest expense is higher than the cash payment for interest.
   d. None of the above is correct.

10. (CO2,3) The reported value of a bond is $500,000, and the company repurchases the bond for $490,000. The company will record:
   a. an extraordinary loss of $10,000.
   b. an extraordinary gain of $10,000.
   c. an ordinary loss of $10,000.
   d. an ordinary gain of $10,000.

Demonstration Problem

Fritz Corporation sold 6% bonds with a face value $500,000 on January 3, 1998. The bonds pay interest on June 30 and December 31 and are to be repaid in 5 years. On the date of the sale, the market rate of interest was 8%.

REQUIRED:

1. Please compute the present value of the bonds.

2. What is the effect of the sale of the bonds on the accounting equation?

3. What is the effect of the first interest payment on the accounting equation?

4. What is the effect of the second interest payment on the accounting equation?

SOLUTIONS TO SELF-TEST

Matching

1. b
2. a
3. f
4. e
5. c
6. d
7. h
8. g

Completion

1. premium
2. amortized
3. extraordinary
4. present value
5. noncurrent
6. Collateral
7. convertible
8. Depreciation

Multiple Choice

1. c
2. b
3. a
4. d
5. b
6. d
7. a
8. c
9. b
10. a

Demonstration Problem

1. Annual interest on the bond is $30,000 ($500,000 X 6%). Therefore, the cash payment each six months is $15,000. Since the market rate of interest is 8% and the bonds are 5-year bonds, the factor from each table will be the factor at 10n, 4% because the bonds pay interest twice a year. Without performing the computation, it can be seen that the bond will sell at a discount because the coupon rate of interest is lower than the market rate of interest.

Table 8A-3	$500,000 X 0.676 =	$338,000
Table 8A-4	$ 15,000 X 8.111 =	121,665
	Present value	$459,665

2. Cash will increase by $459,665. Net Bonds Payable will increase by the same amount: Bonds Payable will be a positive of $500,000, while Bond Discount will be a negative of $40,335.

3. Interest Expense will increase, thus decreasing Retained Earnings, by $18,387 (rounded) ($459,665 X .04). Cash will decrease by $15,000, and Bond Discount will be a positive of $3,387 ($18,387 - $15,000).

4. Interest Expense will increase, thus decreasing Retained Earnings, by $18,522 (rounded) ($463,052 X .04). Cash will decrease by $15,000, and Bond Discount will be a positive of $3,522 ($18,522 - $15,000). The $463,052 is the sum of the original reported value of $459,665 and the bond discount of $3,387 from number 3 above.

CHAPTER 10

SHAREHOLDERS' EQUITY

CHAPTER OVERVIEW

Chapter 10 examines the components of shareholders' equity of a corporation. You will learn about the types of transactions and events that affect these components and study several ratios used to analyze shareholders' equity.

Review of Specific Chapter Objectives

1. Understand why large business firms prefer to organize as corporations.

   ▲ A **corporation** is an entity which is owned by its shareholders and which raises equity capital by selling shares of stock to investors. Each share of stock represents a fractional interest in the issuing company. A **primary advantage of the corporate form of business organization** is the ability to raise large amounts of cash by selling stock to many different individuals and institutions on the major security exchanges.

   ▲ **Stockholders expect to receive dividends or to earn capital gains on their investment.** Dividends are distributions of corporate assets, usually cash, to shareholders. Capital gains (or losses) occur when the shares of stock increase (or decrease) in price while investors own the shares.

   ▲ **Each state has laws governing the formation of corporations:** There is no federal law. The state issues to a new corporation a charter which lists various items, among them the businesses's purpose and the number and types of shares of stock the corporation is allowed to sell.

- ▲ **The most basic type of ownership** is common stock. Common shareholders are residual owners of a corporation. If a business liquidates, then the order of distribution of assets (if any) is creditors, preferred shareholders, common shareholders.

- ▲ **Shareholders' equity, or net assets, has two sources:** invested capital and retained earnings. **Invested capital (usually consisting of par value and paid-in capital)** is the amount received by the corporation upon the sale of its stock to investors. **Retained earnings** is the amount of prior earnings that the firm has not paid to shareholders in the form of dividends.

- ▲ **Shares of stock have the following descriptive terms: authorized, issued, and outstanding. Authorized shares** are the shares that the firm is permitted to issue according to its corporate charter. **Issued and outstanding shares** are those presently held by investors. Please note that all issued shares may not necessarily be outstanding. At times, a business may buy back its own shares from investors in the marketplace. The term "issued" means that the shares of stock have at one time been sold into the marketplace but does not necessarily mean that the shares are currently still in the marketplace.

- ▲ **For legal purposes, the shares of most firms have a par or stated value.** It is usually a very small amount, such as $.25, and bears no relation whatsoever to the dollar amount for which the shares are selling in the marketplace (called the fair market value).

2. Comprehend the types of transactions and events that affect the components of shareholders' equity.

- ▲ There are **three basic transactions which account for most of the changes in shareholders' equity:** sale of stock to investors, recognition of net income or loss, and declaration of cash dividends to shareholders.

- ▲ If **a corporation sells 100,000 shares of its $1.00 par value common stock for $5.00 per share,** then the following happens to the accounting equation: Cash and shareholders' equity both increase by $500,000 (100,000 X $5). There is a further subdivision within shareholders' equity. Par value increases by $100,000 (100,000 X $1) while the remaining $400,000 increases capital in excess of par value. Please note that the corporation may issue stock for noncash assets, too, such as land or equipment.

- ▲ **Net income (loss) represents an increase (decrease) in a firm's shareholders' equity due to its revenues, expenses,**

gains, and losses during the accounting period. Firms prepare **statements of retained earnings** which are reconciliations of the beginning and ending balance in the retained earnings account. The ending balance reflects the net income earned by the firm less net loss incurred and dividends paid over the entire life of the firm.

▲ There are **three dates which are important in the declaration and distribution of cash dividends.** On the date of declaration, the dividend becomes a liability: Retained Earnings is decreased and Dividends Payable is increased by the amount of the dividend. Shareholders who own the stock on the date of record are eligible to receive the dividend. Shareholders who purchase the stock after the date of record but before the date of payment buy the stock "ex dividend," which means "without the dividend." Those purchasers will, however, be eligible to receive the next dividend. On the date of payment, both the liability and cash are reduced by the amount of the dividend.

▲ There are **other, less frequent occurrences which affect shareholders' equity.** Stock dividends are dividends issued to shareholders in the form of shares of stock, not cash. A corporation has outstanding 200,000 shares of common stock and decides to issue a 5% stock dividend when the market price of the stock is $20 per share. The firm will issue 10,000 new shares (200,000 shares X 5%), and the total value of the dividend is $200,000 (10,000 X $20). Retained Earnings will decrease and Invested Capital will increase by $200,000. (Please note that Invested Capital will be further subdivided into par value and capital in excess of par value.) **Only the shareholders' equity section of the accounting equation is affected.** A dollar amount is transferred from Retained Earnings into Invested Capital. Since it is the same dollar amount, **nothing happens to the total of shareholders' equity because of the stock dividend.** A stock dividend gives nothing of present value to the investor when he receives the shares of stock. However, the investor now has more shares of stock which can appreciate in price in the future.

▲ **Stock splits** also increase the number of outstanding shares but, unlike dividends, they do not entail a reduction in retained earnings or an increase in paid-in capital. The description of the firm's stock is changed to reflect the new par value and the number of shares authorized, issued, and outstanding. If a firm had outstanding 500,000 shares of $2.00 par value common stock when the market price was $100 per share, then the following will happen when the firm declares a 2-for-1 stock split: The number of shares will double to 1,000,000, the par value will decrease by half to $1.00, and the market price will decrease by half to $50 per share. **The total of invested capital, $1,000,000, will be exactly the same before and after the split.** Companies often split their stock when the market price becomes so high that small investors cannot afford to buy the stock. Companies usually do not like that only large, institutional investors hold their shares. Harley-Davidson seems to split its stock when the market price stays at approximately $60, and Microsoft Corporation has split its stock during the past several years when the market price has hovered at $120.

▲ If a company buys back its own shares of stock, the **repurchased shares of stock are called treasury stock:** They have issued but not outstanding status. Companies buy back stock for various reasons: to support the stock price, to have available shares for employee stock option plans, and to take off the market shares which could be purchased by a hostile buyer. Wall Street analysts usually view treasury stock purchases very favorably and as a sign of strength for the repurchasing company. **The acquisition of treasury reduces cash and shareholders' equity**, and treasury stock is a contra-equity account (subtracted from shareholders' equity). Consider the following example. A corporation has repurchased 10,000 of its own shares for $30 per share: Cash and shareholders' equity have both decreased by $300,000. If the corporation later sells the same stock for $40 per share, then the following will happen to the accounting equation: Cash will increase by $400,000; Treasury Stock will increase by the original $300,000; and Invested Capital will increase by the difference of $100,000.

▲ **Stock options** are rights to purchase a firm's stock at a specific price over some designated future period and are usually granted as part of the compensation paid to key executives and other employees. There are **several benefits for employees and firms**. First, such options usually highly motivate option holders to improve the performance of the firm. In addition, option holders avoid the downside risk of loss if the stock price declines. Last, companies do not recognize any compensation expense associated with the options under current GAAP. In the year in which options are granted, no compensation expense is recorded. When they are exercised, the company increases Cash and Invested Capital for the appropriate dollar amount. **GAAP for stock options is a hotly debated topic**, and the **FASB currently requires significant disclosures** about options in the notes to the financial statements.

▲ **Firms may issue preferred stock** which has a priority claim over common stock with respect to dividends and in the event of a liquidation of a company's assets. Various features may attach to preferred stock. **Cumulative** means that any dividend not paid to preferred shareholders will not be forever lost: It will be paid in a year in which the firm has money to pay that dividend. **Convertible** indicates that preferred shares may be exchanged for common shares at the preferred shareholders' option.

▲ **Convertible bonds** allow the bondholder to exchange bonds for a specified number of shares of stock. Investors usually view this convertibility feature very favorably. Convertible bonds are an example of hybrid securities which are neither clearly debt nor clearly equity. Just as is true for stock options, the proper accounting for hybrid securities is a matter of sharp debate.

3. Interpret shareholders' equity ratios that are helpful in analyzing financial statements.

▲ **Earnings per share** is such a highly regarded ratio that it is the only ratio required to be reported on the front of a financial statement (the income statement). It **indicates the portion of company income applicable to a single share of common stock.** It is computed by dividing net income available to common shareholders by the weighted average number of common shares outstanding. Consider the following with respect to computing the weighted average number of shares. A company had outstanding 100,000 shares of stock on January 1. On July 1 it issued another 20,000 shares of stock, and on October 1 it bought back 30,000 shares. The weighted average number of shares is computed as follows:

January 1	100,000 X 6/12 =	50,000
July 1	120,000 X 3/12 =	30,000
October 1	90,000 X 3/12 =	22,500
		102,500

Please make sure that the total of the fraction numerators is 12. It is easy to make a mistake in this area!

If net income for the above company is $550,000, then earnings per share is $5.37 (rounded) ($550,000 ÷ 102,500).

If **preferred stock is present in the capital structure, then its dividend must be subtracted from net income before dividing by the weighted average number of common shares.** Using the same example, if the annual preferred dividend is $30,000, then earnings per share is $5.07 (rounded) ($550,000 - $30,000 = $520,000 ÷ 102,500).

▲ The **financial leverage, or debt-to-total-assets, ratio** is computed by dividing total assets into total liabilities. These ratios are widely used by analysts in assessing the risks of debt and equity securities. High financial leverage is associated with lower bond quality ratings and, therefore, higher borrowing costs. The share prices of highly leveraged firms tend to be more volatile than the share prices of firms with lower financial leverage. Just as is true with other ratios, care must be taken when comparing firms in different industries.

- ▲ The **market-to-book-value ratio** is computed by dividing book value per share into market price per share. Market price measures the economic value of the stock while book value reflects the methods used to identify and measure assets and liabilities.

- ▲ The **price-to-earnings ratio** is computed by dividing earnings per share into the market price per share. These ratios are often used to assess growth, risk and earnings quality. **Earnings quality** refers to the sustainability of currently reported earnings in future periods. Firms using conservative methods of income measurement are more likely to be viewed as having higher earnings quality than firms using more liberal income measurement methods.

CHAPTER SELF-TEST

Note: The notation (CO1) means that the question was drawn from chapter objective number one.

Matching

Please write the letters of the following terms in the spaces to the left of the definitions.

a. Authorized shares
b. Common stock
c. Cumulative preferred stock
d. Date of declaration
e. Date of record
f. Issued shares
g. Outstanding shares
h. Par value
i. Retained earnings
j. Treasury stock

_____ 1. (CO1) Shares which have at one time been sold into the marketplace.

_____ 2. (CO2) Shares of a company's own stock which it has repurchased from investors.

_____ 3. (CO1) Most basic type of ownership share.

_____ 4. (CO2) A firm's total of all income earned, losses incurred, and dividends paid.

_____ 5. (CO1) Shares a firm is permitted to sell according to its corporate charter.

_____ 6. (CO2) Date on which is prepared a listing of stock owners who are eligible to receive a dividend.

_____ 7. (CO1) Number of shares which have been sold into and which still are in the marketplace.

_____ 8. (CO2) This type of stock will not forever lose its dividend if the dividend is not declared and paid in a given year.

_____ 9. (CO1) A minimal dollar value assigned to a share of stock when the firm incorporates.

_____ 10. (CO2) Date on which a dividend becomes a liability.

<u>Completion</u>

Please write in the word or words which will complete the sentence.

1. (CO2) A stock ________________________ affects neither assets nor liabilities, but it does affect shareholders' equity.

2. (CO2) A stock ________________________ does not change any part of the accounting equation or any items on financial statements.

3. (CO2) ________________________ are distributions of assets, usually cash, to shareholders.

4. (CO3) ____________________ ____________________ refers to the sustainability of currently reported earnings in future periods.

5. (CO2) Securities which are neither clearly debt nor clearly equity are called ________________ ________________.

6. (CO2) The ________________________ is a document issued to a new corporation by the state in which it incorporates.

7. (CO1) The two sources of shareholders' equity are ________________ ________________ and ________________ ________________.

8. (CO3) The only ratio required to be reported on the front of the income statement is ______________________________.

9. (CO3) The financial leverage ratio is computed by dividing ________________ ________________ into ________________ ________________.

10. (CO2) ____________________ stock has a priority claim on dividends over common shares.

Multiple Choice

Please circle the correct answer.

1. (CO1) In the event of a firm's liquidation, which of the following is the order of preference?
   a. Common shareholders, preferred shareholders, creditors.
   b. Preferred shareholders, common shareholders, creditors.
   c. Creditors, common shareholders, preferred shareholders.
   d. Creditors, preferred shareholders, common shareholders.

2. (CO1) Invested capital usually includes two components, which are:
   a. retained earnings and par value.
   b. retained earnings and paid-in capital.
   c. par value and paid-in capital.
   d. par value and common stock.

3. (CO2) Retained earnings at the beginning of the year was $50,000. Net income for the year totaled $15,000, and dividends declared during the year totaled $5,000. Retained earnings at the end of the year is:
   a. $70,000.
   b. $65,000.
   c. $60,000.
   d. $30,000.

4. (CO2) A company has outstanding 300,000 shares of $2.00 par value common stock. It decides to declare a 5% stock dividend when the market price is $10 per share. Retained earnings will be:
   a. increased by $150,000.
   b. decreased by $150,000.
   c. increased by $ 30,000.
   d. decreased by $ 30,000.

5. (CO2) A company has outstanding 400,000 shares of $5.00 par value common stock. It declares a 2-for-1 stock split at a time when the market price of the stock is $150.00 per share. As a result of the split:
   a. the number of shares outstanding is halved to 200,000.
   b. the par value of $5.00 will remain the same.
   c. the number of shares outstanding remains the same.
   d. the par value of $5.00 will be halved to $2.50.

6. (CO2) A corporation spent $500,000 buying back 100,000 of its own shares. It decided to sell these treasury shares back into the marketplace for $700,000. As a result of the sale:
   a. Treasury Stock increased by $500,000.
   b. Cash decreased by $700,000.
   c. Invested Capital increased by $700,000.
   d. Invested Capital decreased by $200,000.

7. (CO3) On January 1, a company had outstanding 400,000 shares of common stock. It issued another 100,000 shares on April 1, and on October 1 it repurchased 50,000 of those shares. What is the weighted average number of shares to be used in the earnings per share ratio?
   a. 400,000.
   b. 450,000.
   c. 462,500.
   d. 500,000.

8. (CO3) A corporation has outstanding 200,000 shares of preferred stock, each of which receives an annual dividend of $3.00. Net income for the year is $1,500,000, and the weighted average number of common shares outstanding is 500,000. What is earnings per share?
   a. $3.00.
   b. $1.80.
   c. $ .56 (rounded).
   d. $ .34 (rounded).

9. (CO3) The par value of a share of a company's common stock is $5.00. The market price of the stock is $30.00 per share, and earnings per share is $2.25. What is the price-to-earnings ratio?
   a. 00.08.
   b. 02.22.
   c. 06.00.
   d. 13.33.

10. (CO2) Par value stock totals $300,000, and paid-in capital totals $150,000. Retained earnings totals $800,000, while treasury stock totals $100,000. What is total shareholders' equity?
    a. $1,100,000.
    b. $1,150,000.
    c. $1,250,000.
    d. $1,350,000.

Demonstration Problem

Browser Corporation had a Retained Earnings account balance of $950,000 on December 31, 1997. The following transactions occurred during 1998:

a. The corporation declared and paid a cash dividend of $.50 per share on its common stock. Three hundred fifty thousand shares were outstanding on the date of declaration.

b. The corporation declared and distributed a 2% stock dividend when the market price was $30 per share and 350,000 shares were outstanding.

c. For 1998, the corporation incurred a net loss of $20,000.

REQUIRED: Please prepare a statement of retained earnings for 1998 (CO2).

SOLUTIONS TO SELF-TEST

Matching

1. f
2. j
3. b
4. i
5. a
6. e
7. g
8. c
9. h
10. d

Completion

1. dividend
2. split
3. Dividends
4. Earnings quality
5. hybrid securities
6. charter
7. invested capital, retained earnings
8. earnings per share
9. total assets, total liabilities
10. Preferred

Multiple Choice

1. d
2. c
3. c
4. b   300,000 X 5% = 15,000 new shares X $10 = $150,000
5. d
6. a
7. c
8. b
9. d
10. b $300,000 + $150,000 + $800,000 - $100,000

Demonstration Problem

Browser Corporation
Statement of Retained Earnings
For the Year Ended December 31, 1998

Retained earnings, December 31, 1997		$950,000
Deduct:	Net loss during 1998	20,000
	Cash dividends	175,000
	Stock dividends	210,000
Retained earnings, December 31, 1998		$545,000

Cash dividends: 350,000 X $.50 = $175,000
Stock dividends: 350,000 shares X 2% = 7,000 new shares
7000 shares X $30 = $210,000

CHAPTER 11

A FRAMEWORK FOR FINANCIAL STATEMENT ANALYSIS

CHAPTER OVERVIEW

Chapter 11 shows how a comprehensive financial statement analysis can be conducted. It links many of the ratios and analytical concepts that you have studied in previous chapters and also discusses limitations of such analysis.

Review of Specific Chapter Objectives

1. Understand why financial statements are analyzed.

   ▲ **In order for financial information to be useful, it must be interpreted.** A comprehensive set of ratios, in an organized framework, allows the user to make sense of all the financial information reported in the financial statements and, thus, to use the information to make decisions.

   ▲ **Users of financial information may be current or future users.** Examples of users are <u>investors</u>, <u>managers</u>, <u>customers</u>, <u>potential suppliers and creditors</u>, <u>government regulators</u>, <u>employee unions</u>, and <u>public interest and community groups</u>.

2. Know where to obtain financial information.

   ▲ The **major source of financial information** is a <u>firm's annual report</u>. The following are elements of most annual reports:
   a. Management discussion and analysis (may also include a letter from the CEO)
   b. Independent auditor's report (management's statement of responsibility for the financial statements is usually included, too)
   c. Primary financial statements
   d. Secondary financial statements

e. Notes to the financial statements

▲ **Other sources of information include the following:**
a. Reports filed with regulatory agencies (special, quarterly, and annual)
b. Business periodicals (magazines, newspapers, newsletters)
c. Investment advisory services (Standard & Poor, Moody's, etc.)

3. Determine when financial information is comparable; alternatively, learn how to enhance the comparability of financial information that may appear to be noncomparable.

▲ When analyzing financial reports, **one of the first decisions is to identify the basis of comparison.** Data may be compared with the firm's data from prior years, with data from another firm in the same industry, with data from another firm in which the analyst may invest, with industry averages, or with benchmarks or targets.

▲ **If significant unusual events which would distort comparisons have occurred, then the statements may need to be restated.** Such events include, among others, mergers or acquisitions, discontinued operations, changes in accounting principles, and extraordinary items.

▲ **Comparability is enhanced when firms' size, capital structure, and product mix are similar.**

4. Identify, calculate, use, and interpret appropriate ratios.

▲ The **analyst usually performs horizontal and vertical analyses of the financial statements.** Horizontal analysis focuses on changes or growth, year to year, for each major element on the income statement and the balance sheet. Vertical analysis examines the percentage composition of the income statement and the balance sheet: It uses common-size financial statements for this analysis.

▲ **Ratios are usually grouped into broad categories.** Four widely used major headings are liquidity, profitability, capital structure, and investor.

▲ **Liquidity ratios indicate the short-term solvency of the firm.** They **also indicate how effectively the firm is managing its working capital.** The following are commonly used liquidity ratios:
a. Current ratio: current assets ÷ current liabilities
b. Quick ratio: (cash + cash equivalents + accounts receivable) ÷ current liabilities

c. Collection period: accounts receivable ÷ average sales per day. Average sales per day is calculated by dividing sales revenue by 365.

d. Number of days sales in ending inventory: ending inventory ÷ cost of goods sold per day. Cost of goods sold per day is calculated by dividing cost of goods sold by 365.

e. Quality of sales: cash received from customers ÷ sales revenue

f. Accounts receivable as percent of sales: gross accounts receivable ÷ sales revenue

▲ **Profitability ratios measure how profitable a firm is.** This is very important for investors who want to invest in a firm which can return their investment to them. The following are commonly used profitability ratios:

a. Gross profit percentage: gross profit ÷ net sales revenue

b. Operating income percentage: (operating income + extraordinary losses - unusual gains) ÷ sales revenue

c. Net income percentage: (net income + interest expense net of tax) ÷ sales revenue

d. Return on equity: net income ÷ average shareholders' equity

e. Return on assets: (net income + interest expense net of tax) ÷ average total assets

f. Cash return on assets: (cash flow from operating activities + interest paid + taxes paid) ÷ average total assets

g. Quality of income: cash flow from operating activities ÷ operating income

▲ **Capital structure ratios help in assessing a firm's strategies for financing its assets.** Capital structure indicates the relative amounts of debt and equity capital. Percentage composition analysis is the starting point for any analysis of capital structure: It provides a description of the relative amounts of capital obtained from each major source of financing. Current liabilities, long-term debt, deferred taxes and other similar liabilities, and shareholders' equity all will be divided by the total of total liabilities and shareholders' equity. The following ratios are also computed:

a. Financial leverage (or debt to total assets): total liabilities ÷ total assets

b. Cash interest coverage: (cash flow from operating activities + interest paid + taxes paid) ÷ interest paid

c. Times interest earned: earnings before interest and taxes (or EBIT) ÷ interest expense

▲ **Investor ratios all relate to an external dimension of ownership interest:** Most indicate how a firm is performing with regard to the market value of its shares. The following ratios are computed thus:

a. Earnings-per-share: net income ÷ weighted average number of shares outstanding
b. Market-to-book value: market price per share ÷ book value per share
c. Price-to-earnings: market price per share ÷ earnings per share

▲ To summarize, the **financial statement analysis framework includes the following steps:**

1. Identify the purpose and objectives of the analysis.
2. Review the financial statements, notes and audit opinion.
3. Determine whether restatements are necessary to enhance the comparability of the statements.
4. Determine whether the firm's size, capital structure, and product mix are appropriate to proceed with the ratio calculations.
5. Conduct horizontal and vertical analyses of each financial statement, with special emphasis on the income statement.
6. Calculate the basic liquidity ratios.
7. Calculate profitability ratios based on net income and on cash flow from operating activities. Evaluate trends.
8. Evaluate the firm's capital structure with special emphasis on trends in the percentage composition ratios.
9. Examine the firm's market performance using the investor ratios.
10. Examine any inconsistencies in the ratio results. Review notes, and recalculate the ratios.

5. Identify limitations of financial statement analyses.

▲ **Financial statement analysis is limited due to several items.**

▲ **First, GAAP presents some limits.** Managers often have the ability to select favorable accounting methods.

▲ **Second, many major factors affecting profitability and survival of the firm are not included in the financial statements.** A perfect example is human resources. While employees are often a firm's most important asset, a value for employees does not appear on the balance sheet.

▲ **Third, "real" events are often hard to distinguish from the effects of alternative accounting methods or principles.**

▲ **Fourth, financial statement analysis relies on past numbers, and the past may not be a reliable indication of the future.**

CHAPTER SELF-TEST

Note: The notation (CO1) means that the question was drawn from chapter objective number one.

Matching

Please write the letters of the following terms in the spaces to the left of the definitions.

a. Earnings-per-share (EPS)
b. Horizontal analysis
c. Investor ratios
d. Liquidity ratios
e. Price-to-earnings ratio (P/E)
f. Vertical analysis

_____ 1. (CO4) Focuses on year-to-year changes or growth for each major element of a financial statement.

_____ 2. (CO4) Indicate the short-term solvency of a firm.

_____ 3. (CO4) The only ratio required to be reported on the front of a financial statement (the income statement).

_____ 4. (CO4) Indicates the relationship between market prices and earnings.

_____ 5. (CO4) Examines the percentage composition of elements of a financial statement.

_____ 6. (CO4) Indicate how a firm is performing with regard to the market value of its shares.

Completion

Please write in the word or words which will complete the sentence.

1. (CO1) Examples of users of financial statements include ____________________, ____________________, and ____________________.

2. (CO2) A firm must file with the SEC an annual report called the ____________________ report.

3. (CO2) Two business periodicals which are sources of public information about companies are ____________________ and ____________________.

4. (CO2) The part of an annual report which is a narrative providing a qualitative description of the year's highlights is the ______________________________.

5. (CO3) When comparing two companies, comparability is enhanced if ______________________, ______________________, and ______________________ are similar.

6. (CO4) ______________________ financial statements are a tool used in vertical analysis.

7. (CO4) ______________________ ______________________ indicates the relative amounts of debt and equity capital which a firm has.

8. (CO4) The ______________________ ratio is computed by dividing sales revenue into cash received from customers.

9. (CO4) Another name for the return on equity (ROE) ratio is ______________________ ratio.

10. (CO5) The fact that the past is not necessarily a reliable predictor of the future is considered to be a ______________________ of financial statement analysis.

Multiple Choice

Please circle the correct answer.

1. (CO2) Which of the following is an investment advisory service?
   a. Barron's.
   b. Fortune.
   c. Dun & Bradstreet.
   d. Wall Street Journal.

2. (CO3) Which of the following is a basis of comparison for a financial statement analysis?
   a. The prior year.
   b. Another firm in the same industry.
   c. Industry averages.
   d. All of the above are bases for comparison.

3. (CO4) Return on equity and return on assets are both examples of:
   a. liquidity ratios.
   b. profitability ratios.
   c. investor ratios.
   d. capital structure ratios.

4. (CO4) Gross accounts receivable is $300,000, while sales revenue is $500,000. What is the average sales per day?
   a. $6,000.
   b. $1,670.
   c. $1,370.
   d. It cannot be determined from the information given.

5. (CO4) The quality of sales ratio indicates:
   a. the proportion of sales revenue that has generated cash in the current year.
   b. how quickly a firm is "turning" its working capital.
   c. the percentage of sales that remains uncollected.
   d. the relationship between accounts receivable and sales revenue.

6. (CO4) Which ratio indicates the proportion of net income earned on every sales dollar?
   a. Gross profit percentage.
   b. Operating income percentage.
   c. Cash return on assets.
   d. Net income percentage.

7. (CO4) If earnings before interest and taxes are divided by interest expense, then the result is the:
   a. cash interest coverage ratio.
   b. earnings-per-share ratio.
   c. times interest earned ratio.
   d. market-to-book value ratio.

8. (CO4) Net income is $500,000, and the weighted average number of common shares outstanding is 250,000. The market price per share of stock is $20. What is the price-to-earnings ratio?
   a. 10.00.
   b. 2.00.
   c. .50.
   d. .10.

9. (CO4) Net income is $500,000, and the weighted average number of common shares outstanding is 250,000. The market price per share of stock is $20. What is the earnings-per-share ratio?
   a. $10.00.
   b. $ 2.00.
   c. $ .50.
   d. $ .10.

10. (CO4) Current assets total $50,000, while noncurrent assets total $100,000. Current liabilities total $20,000, while noncurrent liabilities total $200,000. What is the financial leverage ratio?
    a. 2.50.
    b. 2.00.
    c. 1.47.
    d. .68.

Demonstration Problem

Below are selected data from Portulaca Corporation:

Net sales	$7,600,000
Gross profit	2,200,000
Operating income	1,300,000
Income taxes	520,000
Net income	780,000
Interest paid	176,000
Total current assets	1,500,000
Accounts receivable	400,000
Total noncurrent assets	4,250,000
Total current liabilities	653,000
Total noncurrent liabilities	2,400,000
Average shareholders' equity	4,500,000
Average total assets	5,600,000
Cash flow from operating activities	325,000
Cash received from customers	680,000
Market price per share	$ 15
Weighted average number of shares outstanding	2,500,000

REQUIRED: Please compute the following ratios:

a. Current ratio

b. Collection period

c. Quality of sales

d. Gross profit percentage

e. Return on equity

f. Cash return on assets

g. Quality of income

h. Financial leverage

i. Cash interest coverage

j. Earnings-per-share

k. Price-to-earnings

SOLUTIONS TO SELF-TEST

Matching

1. b
2. d
3. a
4. e
5. f
6. c

Completion

1. investors, managers, customers, suppliers, creditors, regulators, unions, public interest groups
2. Form 10-K
3. Forbes, Fortune, Business Week, Wall Street Journal, Barron's
4. management discussion and analysis (MDA)
5. size, capital structure, product mix
6. Common-size
7. Capital structure
8. quality of sales
9. return on investment (ROI)
10. limitation

Multiple Choice

1. c
2. d
3. b
4. c
5. a
6. d
7. c
8. a
9. b
10. c

Demonstration Problem

a. $1,500,000 ÷ $653,000 = 2.3

b. $400,000 ÷ $20,822 = 19.21 days

Average sales per day = $7,600,000 ÷ 365 = $20,822

c. $680,000 ÷ $7,600,000 = 8.9%

d. $2,200,000 ÷ $7,600,000 = 28.9%

e. $780,000 ÷ $4,500,000 = 17.3%

f. ($325,000 + $176,000 + $520,000) ÷ $5,600,000 = 18.2%

g. $325,000 ÷ $1,300,000 = 25%

h. ($653,000 + $2,400,000) ÷ ($1,500,000 + $4,250,000) = 53%

i. $780,000 ÷ 2,500,000 shares = $.31

j. $15 ÷ $.31 = 48

NOTE: Please be aware that simply computing the ratios for one year does not give sufficient information for financial statement analysis. These numbers must be compared with other numbers so that comparisons can be made and inferences can be drawn. This problem merely gives practice in computing the various ratios.

CHAPTER 12

ADDITIONAL ISSUES IN LIABILITY REPORTING

CHAPTER OVERVIEW

Chapter 12 consists of two parts, one dealing with leases and one dealing with pension and post-retirement obligations. You will learn about the differences between capital and operating leases and the different effects of buying or leasing an asset. You will learn about the different types of pension plans and the accounting issues involved with defined benefit plans. You will also learn about the issues concerning post-retirement obligations of companies.

Review of Specific Chapter Objectives

1. Distinguish between leases that are ordinary rentals and those that are, in substance, a purchase of assets.
2. Understand how leases impact the measurement of financial position and operating performance.

▲ **A business firm may obtain assets either by purchase or lease,** which is an agreement between the lessor (owner) and lessee (renter) which conveys the right to use the leased property for a designated future period. Leases are limited in their terms only by the creativity of the contracting parties and by, of course, legal concerns.

▲ **Benefits of leasing include the following:**

a. They offer financial flexibility to the lessee because lessors generally do not have the power to impose severe restrictions on the lessee.

b. The lessee may have reduced risk of equipment obsolescence.

c. The lessor may be able to resell or re-lease the asset if there is a well-developed secondary market.

d. Because payments are a set amount, the lessee usually

has reduced financial risk.

▲ Consider a case in which a **company purchases an asset**. The company must use compound interest tables to compute the present value of the payment or payments and record an asset and a liability for the present value. The company must record annual interest expense until the loan is paid off and must record depreciation expense for each year that it owns the asset. It must also make periodic payments on the principal of the loan. On the balance sheet, noncurrent assets and liabilities are both increased. On the income statement, both interest and depreciation expenses are recorded.

▲ Consider a case in which a **company leases an asset**. The first thing to determine is whether the lease is a capital or an operating lease. A **capital lease** is interpreted as if it is essentially a purchase of an asset, whereas an **operating lease** is interpreted as an ordinary rental. A lease is considered to be a capital lease if it meets any one or more of the following four criteria:

a. The lease transfers ownership of the property to the lessee by the end of the lease.
b. The lease gives the lessee an option to purchase the leased asset at a bargain price (called a bargain purchase option). If a company leases a 700 series BMW for three years and is given the option to buy the car for $3,000 at the end of the lease, then that would probably be considered a bargain purchase option.
c. The lease term is equal to 75% or more of the estimated economic life of the leased property. If the economic life of the asset is 8 years and the lease term is 7 years, then that lease meets this criterion.
d. The present value of the lease property (the lease payments) is 90% or more of the fair value of the property at the inception of the lease.

If a lease meets none of these criteria, then it is treated as an operating lease.

▲ If the **lease is a capital lease**, then the lessee will record an asset and a liability at the lower of the fair market value of the property or the present value of the minimum lease payments. The present value of the minimum lease payments must be computed using the compound interest tables. The cost of the asset is systematically expensed, or amortized, and the company must also record interest expense on the liability. Annual payments on the principal must also be made. On the balance sheet, noncurrent assets and liabilities are both increased. On the income statement, both interest and amortization expenses are recorded.

▲ If the **lease is an operating lease**, then the lessee will simply record rent expense for each of the payment periods. No asset or liability is recorded; thus, the asset cost will not be amortized because the lessee has not capitalized the cost of the asset.

▲ **Whether the lease is an operating or a capital lease can have a dramatic effect on financial ratios.** Ratios using net income, total assets, or debt in their calculations will be affected. Thus, return on assets, the debt-to-assets ratio, and earnings per share will all appear less favorable in the earlier years of a capital lease. Operating leases are often called "off-balance-sheet" financing because neither an asset nor a liability is recorded. **A company with any type of lease is required to disclose substantial details of the lease in the notes to the financial statements.**

3. Know the difference between defined contribution and defined benefit pension plans.

▲ **A defined contribution plan** specifies the periodic amount that the firm must contribute to a pension fund. The employer's only obligation is to make the agreed-upon contributions to the plan. The employee bears all the risks and rewards. Accounting for these plans is straightforward and noncontroversial.

▲ **A defined benefit plan** specifies the benefits that employees will receive at retirement. The employer assumes all the risks and rewards associated with pension fund investments. You can see that the employer knows how much he must pay to an employee in the future but must estimate and make assumptions about investments and actuarial concerns so that he can invest enough to have that required future amount available. These types of plans are popular in U.S. industries having strong labor union representation.

▲ It is **important to differentiate between the employer and the pension fund.** The employer makes contributions to the pension fund, and the fund makes payments to retirees. (Some analysts do not regard the fund as a separate entity and would like to see the employer firm and the fund consolidated for reporting purposes.)

4. Appreciate the impact of retirement benefit liabilities on reported financial position and operating results.

▲ An **employer must estimate future payments to retirees and discount the payments to present values using an appropriate rate of interest.** The choice of a discount rate is critical. Many companies use overly optimistic discount rates, and surveys show that these companies are severely underfunded in their pension plans. Note the **following rule of thumb:** A 1% variation in the assumed discount rate will cause about a 20% variation in the valuation of pension obligations.

▲ There are **three possible present value measurements.** The **vested benefit obligation** indicates amounts to which employees have irrevocable rights. The **accumulated benefit obligation** shows the amount of benefits that employees have earned to date, based on current salary levels. The **projected benefit obligation** shows the amount of benefits that employees have earned to date, based on expected future salary levels. Managers and analysts often disagree about which of these best represents a firm's pension obligation. **Present accounting standards are a compromise,** disclosing two types of pension costs along with extensive supplementary disclosures in the notes to the financial statements.

▲ The following are **components of pension expense:**

a. **Service cost,** which is the value of future pension benefits that employees have earned during the current year

b. **Interest cost** on the projected benefit obligation

c. **Return on plan assets,** based on anticipated, not actual, return. The return can be either a positive or a negative number, depending on how the investments have done

d. **Other items (net),** such as amortization of prior pension cost, obligations resulting from changes in pension benefits, and revision in assumptions underlying the pension valuation, among others

▲ **Pension reporting involves two types of assumptions:** actuarial (employee turnover, services lives, longevity, etc.), which are fairly standardized and noncontroversial; and economic (discount rate and return on plan assets), which stir up much controversy. The biggest problem seems to be with the discount rate used by companies. As noted above, a 1% difference in the discount rate can cause a 20% difference in the pension obligation.

5. Understand the key assumptions necessary to measure postretirement obligations and expenses.

▲ **SFAS No. 106 requires that firms currently report their obligations to provide future nonpension postretirement benefits and accrue the expenses during the years that employees provide service.** Adoption of this new standard in 1993 reduced profits at the 100 largest U.S. corporations by about 33%.

▲ There are **two major differences between pension and nonpension benefits.** First, the accumulated postretirement benefit obligation measures the present value of the future benefits that employees and retirees have earned to date. Second, the fair market values of the plan assets are minor, relative to the accumulated benefit obligation.

▲ **Cost components for nonpension expenses follow the same format as those for pension costs.** The service cost represents the amount of the accumulated benefit obligation earned by employees over the current year. The interest cost is the beginning-of-the-year obligation multiplied by the discount rate. The return on plan assets is only a minor offset to the other components because the benefits are not substantially funded.

▲ As is true for pension benefits, the **FASB requires significant disclosures for nonpension postretirement benefits in the notes to the financial statements.**

CHAPTER SELF-TEST

Note: The notation (CO1) means that the question was drawn from chapter objective number one.

Matching

Please write the letters of the following terms in the spaces to the left of the definitions.

a. Accumulated benefit obligation
b. Capital lease
c. Defined benefit plan
d. Defined contribution plan
e. Operating lease
f. Projected benefit obligation

_____ 1. (CO1,2) Lease in which the lessee records an asset and a liability for the leased asset.

_____ 2. (CO4) Shows the amount of pension benefits earned by employees, based on current salary levels.

_____ 3. (CO3) Type of pension plan in which the employer assumes all of the risks and rewards associated with the pension fund investments.

_____ 4. (CO1,2) Lease for which the lease payments are recorded as rent expense.

_____ 5. (CO4) Shows the amount of pension benefits earned by employees, based on future salary levels.

_____ 6. (CO3) Type of pension plan in which is specified the periodic amount that a firm must contribute to a pension fund.

Completion

Please write in the word or words which will complete the sentence.

1. (CO1,2) With respect to leases, the owner of the leased property is called the ______________________, and the renter is called the ____________________.

2. (CO1,2) A ____________________ lease is interpreted as if it is essentially a purchase of an asset.

3. (CO1,2) One of the criteria for a capital lease states that a lease is to be capitalized if the least term is equal to __________ or more of the estimated economic life of the leased property.

4. (CO1,2) Operating leases are often referred to as ____ financing.

5. (CO3) With a defined contribution pension plan, the ________________________ bears all of the risks and rewards of the investment performance of the pension fund.

6. (CO4) The ________________________ benefit obligation indicates the amount to which employees have irrevocable rights, even if they leave the firm prior to retirement.

7. (CO4) One of the components of pension expense is the ________________________ cost computed on the ________________________ benefit obligation.

8. (CO4) The major controversies about pensions concern the ________________________ assumptions, particularly the assumed interest rate used to discount future pension benefits.

Multiple Choice

Please circle the correct answer.

1. (CO4) Which of the following is NOT a component of pension expense?
   a. Accumulated benefit obligation.
   b. Interest cost.
   c. Service cost.
   d. Return on plan assets.

2. (CO5) Which of the following statements regarding post-retirement nonpension benefits is correct?
   a. Reporting used to be on the accrual basis, but current standards require the cash basis.
   b. Cost components for nonpension expenses are very different from those for pension expenses.
   c. Return on plan assets is a major offset to other cost components for nonpension expenses.
   d. Reporting used to be on the cash basis, but current standards require the accrual basis.

3. (CO1,2) Which of the following is NOT one of the four criteria for determining whether a lease should be capitalized?
   a. The lease transfers ownership of the property to the lessee by the end of the lease.
   b. The present value of the lease property is 80% or more of the fair value of the property at the inception of the lease.
   c. The lease term is equal to 75% or more of the estimated economic life of the leased property.
   d. The lease gives the lessee an option to purchase the leased asset at a bargain price.

4. (CO1,2) A company leased a piece of equipment with a fair market value of $100,000. The present value of the lease payments is $96,000. The equipment has an economic life of 10 years, and the lease period is 7 years. The equipment reverts to the lessor at the end of the lease, and there is no bargain purchase option. Is the lease a capital lease?
   a. Yes, because the lessor gets the equipment back at the end of the lease.
   b. Yes, because the lease term is equal to the appropriate percentage of the estimated economic life of the asset.
   c. Yes, because the present value of the lease property is 90% or more of the fair value of the equipment.
   d. No. The lease is an operating lease.

5. (CO1,2) A company leased a piece of equipment with a fair market value of $100,000. The present value of the lease payments is $89,000. The equipment has an economic life of 10 years, and the lease period is 7 years. The equipment reverts to the lessor at the end of the lease, and there is no bargain purchase option. Is the lease a capital lease?
   a. Yes, because the lessor gets the equipment back at the end of the lease.
   b. Yes, because the lease term is equal to the appropriate percentage of the estimated economic life of the asset.
   c. Yes, because the present value of the lease property is 90% or more of the fair value of the equipment.
   d. No. The lease is an operating lease.

6. (CO3) Which of the following statements is correct?
   a. A defined benefit pension plan puts all the risks and rewards on the employer.
   b. A defined benefit pension plan puts all the risks and rewards on the employee.
   c. A defined contribution pension plan puts all the risks and rewards on the employee.
   d. None of the above statements is correct.

7. (CO4) Which of the following statements about components of pension expense is correct?
   a. Interest cost is computed on the accumulated benefit obligation.
   b. Interest cost is computed on the projected benefit obligation.
   c. Return on plan assets is based on the actual return.
   d. None of the above statements is correct.

8. (CO1,2) Which of the following statements about leases is correct?
   a. Lessors generally have the power to impose strict restrictions on lessees.
   b. A lease increases the lessee's risk of equipment obsolescence.
   c. A lease generally decreases the lessee's financial risk.
   d. A lease generally increases the lessee's financial risk.

<u>Demonstration Problem</u>

Salvia Corporation has just signed a lease with Purple Heart Company. The following are data related to the lease:

Annual payments at year-end, $30,000
8-year economic life
12% borrowing rate
Straight-line benefit pattern
No residual value
7-year lease term
Fair market value of the asset, $140,000

REQUIRED:
1. What kind of lease is this for Salvia Corporation? Why?

2. What are the financial statement effects for Salvia for the first year of the lease?

SOLUTIONS TO SELF-TEST

Matching

1. b
2. a
3. d
4. e
5. f
6. c

Completion

1. lessor, lessee
2. capital
3. 75%
4. off-balance-sheet
5. employee
6. vested
7. interest, projected
8. economic

Multiple Choice

1. a
2. d
3. b
4. c
5. d
6. a
7. b
8. c

Demonstration Problem

1. The lease is a capital lease. While the asset apparently reverts to the lessor at the end of the lease and there is no bargain purchase option, the lease term is more than 75% of the economic life of the asset. In addition, the present value of the lease payments is more than 90% of the fair market value of the lease property. The present value equals $136,920 (4.564 X $30,000), which is greater than $126,000 (90% X $140,000).

2. Financial statement effects are the following:
   a. Leased Assets and Lease Obligations are increased by $136,920.
   b. Amortization Expense increases and Leased Assets decreases by $19,560 ($136,920 ÷ 7 years).
   c. Interest Expense and Lease Obligations both increase by $16,430 (rounded) ($136,920 X 12%).
   d. Lease Obligations and Cash both decrease by $30,000.

Total lease-related expenses are:	$19,560
	16,430
	$35,990

The lease obligation at year-end is:	$136,920
Add: interest expense	16,430
Less: lease payment	30,000
	$123,350

The value of the leased asset is:	$136,920
Less: amortization	19,560
	$117,360

CHAPTER 13

REPORTING ISSUES FOR AFFILIATED AND INTERNATIONAL COMPANIES

CHAPTER OVERVIEW

Chapter 13 consists of two parts, one dealing with consolidated financial statements and one dealing with international accounting. You will learn about the reasons for reporting consolidated statements and the issues involved in the preparation of such statements. You will learn about important issues for companies conducting business in the international arena and how foreign currency fluctuations affect the financial reporting of such companies.

Review of Specific Chapter Objectives

1. Understand the reasons for reporting consolidated financial statements.

▲ **Most large firms grow by a combination of internal and external expansion.** A business combination, a form of external expansion, is attractive for several reasons:

a. External expansion is often less costly than purchasing new assets and competing for customers.
b. The acquired firm may offer advantages such as a network of suppliers and a good work force.
c. The combination may enable the firms to eliminate duplicate facilities or yield economies of scale.
d. The buyer company may improve management of the acquired firm's assets and thus improve profits.
e. The combination may permit a firm to diversify quickly.

▲ The **rapid pace of technological change in communications** has created linkages between industries previously considered to be unrelated.

▲ **Business combinations occur in a variety of ways.** With a merger, a buyer acquires either the stock or the assets and liabilities of an investee firm, whereupon the investee ceases to exist as a separate corporation. With a consolidation, a new corporation is created to acquire the stock or net assets of two or more existing companies, whereupon the original companies cease to exist as separate corporations. In an acquisition, a buyer acquires more than 50% of the voting stock of an investee firm: The buyer is the parent, and the investee firm is the subsidiary of the parent.

▲ **Acquisitions offer several advantages over mergers and consolidations.** The required investment by the parent may be reduced substantially. The parent has only limited liability for the subsidiary's debts. It is relatively easy for the parent to increase or decrease its investment by buying or selling the subsidiary's shares.

▲ **A parent company and the firms it influences or controls** are called affiliated companies.

2. Appreciate how affiliated firms construct and report their consolidated financial statements.

▲ **When one firm acquires the stock of another firm, the value of the resources paid by the parent is used to measure the historical cost of the parent's investment.** The parent is assumed to control the affiliate.

▲ **If the parent pays for the investee more than the value of the investee's net assets, then the difference is accounted for as goodwill.** If Jerry Corporation pays $900,000 for Ceil Corporation, which has net assets of $700,000, then there is internally generated goodwill of $200,000. Jerry Corporation's account, "Investments in Affiliates," will increase by $900,000, and Cash will decrease by $900,000. Ceil Corporation's balance sheet will be unaffected by the acquisition.

▲ **GAAP requires that Jerry Corporation's subsequent financial statements be prepared on a consolidated basis.** Consolidated financial statements report the combined financial position, cash flows, and operating results for all firms under the parent company's control. Consolidation is mainly a process of adding together the financial statement elements of the parent and its subsidiaries, with certain adjustments.

▲ The **balance of the investment account of the parent company must be eliminated** because a firm does not report an investment in its own shares as an asset on the balance sheet. The **investee's shareholders' equity must be**

eliminated because its stock is not considered to be outstanding. The **investee's net assets are revalued.**

- ▲ **While assets and liabilities will probably be higher on the consolidated balance sheet, the shareholders' equity will be the same before and after consolidation.** This is due to the fact that the subsidiary's shareholders' equity has been eliminated.

- ▲ If **the parent does not own 100% of the subsidiary's stock,** then the book value of the outstanding shares of the subsidiary will appear on the consolidated financial statements as "minority interest in consolidated subsidiaries."

- ▲ **After the acquisition date, the parent will often use the equity method of accounting for its investment in affiliated firms.** This method requires that the parent recognize its share of the subsidiary's subsequent income or loss and recognize any dividends paid by the subsidiary as a reduction of the investment. If the subsidiary has net income, then both Investment in Subsidiary and Income from Investments will increase. When the subsidiary pays dividends, Cash will increase and Investment in Subsidiary will decrease. When goodwill is amortized, both Investment in Subsidiary and Income from Investments are decreased.

- ▲ There are **numerous transactions between affiliated firms that require further adjustment** as a part of the consolidation process. Intercompany receivables and payables must be eliminated, as must intercompany sales. Unrealized inventory profits are removed from the carrying value of the inventory.

- ▲ **Ratios are affected by a company's consolidation with another company,** and analysts must be careful to consider the effects of consolidations on such ratios.

- ▲ The **FASB has initiated a study of principles and assumptions which underlie consolidated financial statements.** Two issues concern the development of a measure of control for purposes of including an investee in the consolidation and the extent to which consolidation may impair the usefulness of financial statements. With respect to the latter, the FASB realizes that aggregations of information cause a loss of information.

3. Understand how foreign exchange rate fluctuations affect the financial reporting of transactions conducted in foreign currencies.

- ▲ **International trade has become big business for U.S. firms as they seek worldwide markets and suppliers.** Foreign currency transactions create receivables or payables that must be settled in a foreign currency. The balances are denominated in the foreign currency.

- ▲ When a **U.S. firm collects an accounts receivable paid in a foreign currency,** it must sell the foreign currency at the current foreign exchange rate between the U.S. dollar and the foreign currency. When a **U.S. firm makes payment on an account payable in a foreign currency,** it must buy the foreign currency at the exchange rate.

- ▲ **Direct foreign exchange rates** quote the number of U.S. dollars required for one unit of a foreign currency. **Indirect quotations** indicate the number of foreign currency units required for one U.S. dollar.

- ▲ A **spot rate** is the rate of exchange for immediate delivery of foreign currencies. A **forward rate** is the rate of exchange for future delivery of foreign currencies. The market in which foreign currencies are bought and sold for future delivery is called a currency forward market. **Firms contract to buy or sell in the forward market** in order to hedge, or protect, against the risks of foreign exchange rate fluctuations.

- ▲ **Sales or purchases are recorded using the spot rate on the date of sale.** If the spot rate has changed on the date of payment, then the firm will have a foreign currency loss or gain, depending on which direction the spot rate moved. In order to protect against such gains or losses, a firm may sign a hedging contract with a foreign exchange broker. In such a case, the firm will have a hedging expense, which reduces Retained Earnings, in order to protect itself against a possible larger loss.

- ▲ **Besides hedging foreign currency-denominated receivables or payables,** firms often hedge commitments to engage in future transactions, such as purchase commitments, sales agreements, and employment contracts.

4. Determine how financial statements prepared initially in foreign currencies are translated to U.S. dollars.

- ▲ **A foreign subsidiary of a U.S. firm prepares its financial statements in its functional currency,** the currency in which it transacts its business. The **U.S. parent firm uses U.S. dollars,** making it necessary to translate the subsidiary's financial statements to U.S. dollars.

- ▲ **Foreign exchange rates between the U.S. firm and its subsidiary must be used to translate into U. S. dollars the elements of the subsidiary's financial statements.** The average exchange rate is used to translate income statement items. The current exchange rate is used to translate assets and liabilities. Various historical exchange rates are used to translate the balances of invested capital, beginning retained earnings, and dividends.

▲ **A translation adjustment is often needed** because not all balance sheet elements are translated at the same exchange rate. The interpretation of the translation adjustment is a matter of continuing controversy.

5. Appreciate the wide diversity of international accounting practices.

▲ **A country's accounting standards often reflect the characteristics of the society and business community in which they have evolved.** Diversity arises because of legal system influences, financial structure influences, and taxation influences.

▲ Countries have very different ways of accounting for certain items, such as goodwill, consolidation policy, leases, pensions, and departures from historical cost. For example, while the United States records goodwill as an asset and amortizes it over time, England writes it off immediately to shareholders' equity.

▲ **In order to promote harmonization of standards throughout the world business community,** the International Accounting Standards Committee (IASC) was formed in 1973. It has issued to date over 30 International Accounting Standards. The effectiveness of the IASC is limited by several issues: The committee has no power to enforce its standards, and the standards themselves usually fail to agree on a single method of accounting. U.S. accounting standards require more comprehensive disclosures than do other nations' standards, but other nations argue that "more is not necessarily better."

CHAPTER SELF-TEST

Note: The notation (CO1) means that the question was drawn from chapter objective number one.

Matching

Please write the letters of the following terms in the spaces to the left of the definitions.

a. Acquisition
b. Average exchange rate
c. Consolidation
d. Current exchange rate
e. Forward rate
f. Merger
g. Spot rate

_____ 1. (CO1) Form of business combination in which a buyer firm acquires either the stock or the assets and liabilities of an investee firm, which ceases to exist as a separate firm.

_____ 2. (CO4) Rate used to translate income statement items.

_____ 3. (CO3) Rate of exchange for immediate delivery of foreign currencies.

_____ 4. (CO4) Rate used to translate asset and liability items.

_____ 5. (CO1) Form of business combination in which a buyer acquires more than 50% of the voting stock of an investee firm, thereby controlling the investee.

_____ 6. (CO3) Rate of exchange for future delivery of foreign currencies.

_____ 7. (CO1) Form of business combination in which a new corporation is created to acquire the stock or net assets of two or more existing companies.

Completion

Please write in the word or words which will complete the sentence.

1. (CO1) _______________________ expansion occurs as firms take over, or merge with, other existing firms.

2. (CO1) A _______________________ occurs when a firm expands by taking over existing corporations.

3. (CO1) A buyer firm is called the ____________________ company while the investee firm continues to exist and operates as a ____________________.

4. (CO2) If a buyer firm acquires less than 100% of another company's stock, then the book value of the remaining outstanding shares will appear on the financial statements with the label ____________________.

5. (CO2) After the acquisition, a parent company uses the ____________________ method of accounting for its investment in affiliated firms.

6. (CO3) The ____________________ exchange rate quotes the number of U.S. dollars required for one unit of a foreign currency.

7. (CO3) Protecting against the risks of exchange rate fluctuations is called ____________________.

8. (CO4) The currency in which a firm conducts its business is called the ____________________ currency.

9. (CO4) Financial statements of a company's foreign subsidiaries must be ____________________ into U.S. dollars so that consolidated financial statements can be prepared.

10. (CO5) To promote harmonization of accounting standards, the ____________________ was formed in 1973.

Multiple Choice

Please circle the correct answer.

1. (CO1) A firm's growth by investing in new plant and equipment, research, and other productive assets is called:
   a. internal expansion.
   b. external expansion.
   c. business combinations.
   d. mergers.

2. (CO2) A firm paid $200,000 in cash and $300,000 in stock to buy another firm with net assets of $450,000. This indicates that:
   a. the firm overpaid for the purchased company.
   b. the purchased firm had $50,000 of internally generated goodwill.
   c. the purchased firm had $500,000 of internally generated goodwill.
   d. the net assets of the purchased firm had been recorded incorrectly.

3. (CO2) When consolidated financial statements are prepared:
   a. the balance of the investment account of the parent company must be eliminated.
   b. the shareholders' equity of the purchased company must be eliminated.
   c. the net assets of the purchased company are revalued.
   d. All of the above statements are correct.

4. (CO2) A firm is using the equity method of accounting for an investment in a company of which it owns 100%. When the investee company reports net income of $1,000,000:
   a. the parent company will increase its own Cash account by $1,000,000.
   b. the parent company will decrease its Investment in Subsidiary account by $1,000,000.
   c. the parent company will increase its Investment in Subsidiary account by $1,000,000.
   d. the parent company will decrease its Income from Investments account by $1,000,000.

5. (CO2) A firm is using the equity method of accounting for an investment in a company of which its owns 100%. When the investee company pays dividends of $200,000:
   a. the parent company will decrease its own Cash account by $200,000.
   b. the parent company will increase its own Cash account by $200,000.
   c. the parent company will increase its Investment in Subsidiary account by $200,000.
   d. the parent company will increase its Income from Investments account by $200,000.

6. (CO2) Which of the following is true with respect to consolidated financial statements of a parent firm?
   a. Intercompany receivables and payables must be eliminated.
   b. Intercompany sales must be eliminated.
   c. Unrealized inventory profits must be removed from the carrying value of the inventory.
   d. All of the above statements are correct.

7. (CO3) A U.S. firm has sold on account merchandise of $100,000 to an English firm. On the date of the sale, the spot rate is $1.42. On the date of payment, the spot rate is $1.40. On the date of the sale, the U.S. firm will:
   a. record a receivable of $140,000.
   b. record a receivable of $142,000.
   c. record a foreign currency loss of $2,000.
   d. record a foreign currency gain of $2,000.

8. (CO3) A U.S. firm has sold on account merchandise of $100,000 to an English firm. On the date of the sale, the spot rate is $1.42. On the date of payment, the spot rate is $1.44. On the date of payment, the U.S. firm will:
   a. record a receivable of $140,000.
   b. record a receivable of $144,000.
   c. record a foreign currency loss of $2,000.
   d. record a foreign currency gain of $2,000.

9. (CO4) Which of the following is true with respect to translation of foreign currency financial statements?
   a. The current exchange rate is used to translate income statement items.
   b. The average exchange rate is used to translate asset and liability items.
   c. The current exchange rate is used to translate asset and liability items.
   d. The current exchange rate is used to translate invested capital, beginning retained earnings, and dividends.

10. (CO5) Which of the following give rise to accounting diversity on an international scale?
   a. Taxation influences.
   b. Legal system influences.
   c. Financial structure influences.
   d. All of the above influence accounting diversity.

Demonstration Problem

Meadows Corporation purchased merchandise from Mountains Export, a Swiss firm. According to the terms of the transaction, Meadows must pay 10,000 Swiss francs to Mountains Export in 30 days. The spot rate on the date of the purchase was $0.70.

1. Please discuss the effects of this transaction on Meadows's accounting equation.

2. On the date of payment, the spot rate stood at $0.69. What is the effect of the payment on the accounting equation?

3. What would have been the effects if the spot rate had been $0.72 on the date of payment?

SOLUTIONS TO SELF-TEST

Matching

1. f
2. b
3. g
4. d
5. a
6. e
7. c

Completion

1. External
2. business combination
3. parent, subsidiary
4. minority interest in consolidated subsidiaries
5. equity
6. direct
7. hedging
8. functional
9. translated
10. International Accounting Standards Committee

Multiple Choice

1. a
2. b
3. d
4. c
5. b
6. d
7. b
8. d
9. c
10. d

Demonstration Problem

1. Meadows will record purchases and an account payable of $7,000 ($10,000 X $0.70). Purchases, an expense account, will reduce Retained Earnings, while Accounts Payable will increase liabilities by the same amount. Only the right side of the accounting equation will be affected.

2. Since the spot rate has fallen, Meadows will have a foreign currency gain. Accounts Payable will decrease by the full $7,000; Cash will decrease by $6,900 ($10,000 X $0.69); and Foreign Currency Gain, which will increase Retained Earnings, will increase by the difference, $100.

3. Since the spot rate has risen, Meadows will have a foreign currency loss. Accounts Payable will decrease by the full $7,000; Cash will decrease by $7,200 ($10,000 X $0.72); and Foreign Currency Loss, which will decrease Retained Earnings, will increase by the difference, $200.

CHAPTER 14

ADDITIONAL DIMENSIONS OF FINANCIAL REPORTING

CHAPTER OVERVIEW

Chapter 14 addresses a variety of issues. It discusses how a firm records accounting changes and how it reports segment information. The parts of annual reports are discussed, as are the reports which a firm must file with the SEC. Finally, the chapter discusses the efficient market hypothesis and the two major roles of financial accounting.

Review of Specific Chapter Objectives

1. Interpret the financial statements of firms that have undertaken accounting changes.

   ▲ There are **three types of accounting changes:** a change in accounting principle, a change in accounting estimate, and a change in reporting entity.

   ▲ **A company should be consistent from period to period in principles used,** but firms do sometimes change from one principle to another. The **general rule** requires a cumulative effect adjustment. In the year of change, account balances are restated to show those amounts that would have appeared if the new method had been used all along. A common example is in the area of depreciation. Assume that a company has used sum-of-the-years'-digits depreciation for two years, resulting in a total in the Accumulated Depreciation account of $5,000. At the beginning of year three, the company decides to switch to straight-line for the asset. If the company had used straight-line for the first two years, then the total in the Accumulated Depreciation account would have been $2,000. Remember that Depreciation Expense reduces

Retained Earnings; so, Retained Earnings in our example is $3,000 ($5,000 - $2,000) too low, and Accumulated Depreciation is $3,000 too high. To adjust in the year of the change, the firm will record a $3,000 increase in the account titled "Cumulative Effect of Change in Accounting Principle" (which will increase Retained Earnings) and a $3,000 decrease in Accumulated Depreciation. The "Cumulative Effect..." account will appear as the last item at the bottom of the income statement. **GAAP requires note disclosure of what net income would have been in the current and prior years had the new method been used**, referred to by most accountants as pro forma amounts.

▲ There is an **exception to the general rule.** Some changes are accounted for retroactively, meaning that prior years' financial statements are restated to reflect the use of the new method. Remember that with the general rule, only the current year's statements are restated. The retroactive approach is used in the following situations:

a. A change **from LIFO** to another inventory method
b. A change in the method of accounting for **long-term construction contracts**
c. A change to or from the full-cost method by firms in the **extractive industries**
d. A change made by a firm **issuing financial statements to the public for the first time**
e. When required as part of the transition process for a **new FASB method**

Restating prior years' statements is done sparingly because the appearance of different sets of numbers may erode public confidence in financial reporting.

▲ **Changes in accounting estimates are accounted for currently and prospectively**, meaning that they are included in the year of the change and future years, if appropriate. Prior years' statements are NOT restated. There are so many estimates used in accounting that restating every time a change in estimate occurred would be a nightmare. The effects of changes in accounting estimates on net income must be disclosed in the notes to the financial statements. If there is a change in an estimate which is part of the depreciation calculation, then the **new depreciation expense** is calculated by doing the following: Salvage value is subtracted from the book value of the asset, and the difference is divided by the remaining estimated useful life.

▲ **A change in reporting entity occurs when a firm changes the specific subsidiaries included in its consolidated financial statements.** Such changes are accounted for retroactively, meaning that prior years' financial statements are restated, thus ensuring comparability of the financial statements.

2. Analyze information about business segments.

▲ **All publicly held corporations are required to report certain disclosures about segments in notes to the financial statements.** An industry segment is a component of a firm that provides a product or service, or a group of related products or services, to unaffiliated customers. In identifying segments, factors to consider include the underlying nature of the product or service, the production process, markets, and the marketing process. Segment data can help users of financial statements to assess risk and future trends.

▲ **For each major segment, a firm must report the following:**
  a. Revenue, which includes sales to unaffiliated customers and transfers to other segments
  b. Operating profit or loss, calculated by subtracting a segment's operating expenses from its revenue. This does not include an allocation of general corporate expenses
  c. Identifiable assets, which are assets used exclusively by the segment and a share of the assets used jointly with other segments; again, an allocation of general corporate assets is not included
  d. Other disclosures, including depreciation expense and capital expenditures

▲ A firms' **foreign operations** consist of those revenue-producing activities located outside the firm's home country. Disclosure of revenue, operating profit or loss, and identifiable assets must be made for both foreign and domestic operations. Sales outside the home country are called export sales and must be disclosed. Information about foreign operations and export sales is particularly helpful in assessing a firm's risk.

▲ **Firms are required to disclose if sales to a single customer exceed 10% of revenue.** The customer's industry must be disclosed.

3. Describe annual and interim reports.

▲ **In addition to the financial statements and the related notes, a firm's annual report includes these elements:**
  a. An introductory letter written by the chief executive officer
  b. A review of the firm's types of businesses
  c. A financial summary for each of the five or ten most recent years
  d. Management's discussion and analysis, which contains an analysis of past performance and known trends and which identifies the underlying economic causes of the

observed trends
e. The auditor's report
f. Management's statement of responsibility for preparation of financial statements and for maintaining an adequate system of internal controls
g. Quarterly financial data
h. Quarterly stock price and dividend data
i. A listing of officers and directors

▲ **Two types of forward-looking information are also presented** in annual reports. Management may know of existing circumstances which will have an impact on future operations. Management might also comment on anticipated trends and their effect on the firm's future.

▲ **In an effort to give timely information to users, all publicly held corporations, and many closely held companies, report financial information on an interim basis throughout the year.** Most often, quarterly information is presented. Interim statements are highly abbreviated and contain limited note disclosures. In addition, they are not audited.

▲ While **interim statement are prepared based on the same accounting principles as are used in the annual statements,** there are two exceptions: They frequently require use of additional estimates (inventory may be estimated, not counted physically), and some costs expensed in the annual report are not immediately expensed for the interim report if they clearly benefit more than one interim period.

4. Identify reports filed with the Securities and Exchange Commission.

▲ **Firms must file with the SEC a 10-K report** which contains virtually all the information included in the annual report plus some additional disclosures about litigation, executive compensation, and shareholdings by officers and directors.

▲ **Firms must also file with the SEC 10-Q reports** which include a firm's quarterly financial statements plus additional disclosures about litigation and defaults on debt securities.

5. Explain the efficient market hypothesis and its implications for accounting.

▲ The **efficient market hypothesis (EMH) states that publicly available information is fully reflected in share prices.** Once a corporation releases information, that information is quickly and unbiasedly reflected in share prices. The implication is that a trading strategy based on such information will not be particularly successful.

▲ While there is **considerable evidence that share prices react very quickly (within hours) to accounting information,** several studies have shown that a small portion of the price change associated with an earnings announcement occurs during the 60 days following the announcement. The latter price change is smaller than the transaction costs, and a net profit could not be made.

▲ **Acceptance of the EMH has the following implications for corporate managers and investors.** Managers should realize that they should not attempt to affect share price by using accounting ploys to influence reported earnings. Individual investors should realize that they are unable to earn abnormal profits by developing trading strategies based on publicly available information.

▲ **Rejection of the EMH has the following implications for corporate managers and investors.** Managers will feel that they can affect share price by using accounting ploys to influence reported earnings. Individual investors will feel that share prices do not necessarily reflect all publicly available information and will scour financial statements and other information in order to identify underpriced securities.

▲ **Acceptance of the EMH does not undermine the usefulness of financial statements.** All investors benefit from disclosure of financial information. Financial statements help stock markets identify relatively efficient companies and also can be used in corporate buyouts. Financial statements can be very useful in valuing closely held companies which are not publicly traded and can be used in credit-granting decisions and labor negotiations.

▲ Some **critics of the EMH recommend purchasing low P/E stocks.** (Remember that the price-to-earnings ratio is computed by dividing the market price of a share of stock by the earnings per share.) This may or may not be good strategy because P/E ratios vary among firms for several reasons. First, firms use different accounting principles which affect EPS. Second, firms have variations in earnings growth which affect EPS. Third, a firm may have a transitory component of income in a given year, and this will certainly have an effect on EPS.

6. Describe the two major roles of financial accounting.

▲ **Financial accounting plays two roles.** The first is to provide information useful for economic decision making. This role is emphasized by the FASB when it develops GAAP. The **two primary qualities that make accounting information useful** are relevance, which refers to an item's capacity to make a difference in a decision, and reliability, which refers to an item's integrity (does the item measure what it purports to measure?).

- ▲ The **second role** is to serve as basis for engaging in contracts. Firms enter into contracts defined in terms of numbers from the financial statements: Changing the accounting principles used to prepare the statements alters the terms of contracts.

- ▲ **The FASB rejects the approach that it should consider the economic consequences of their accounting principle choices.** It seeks "truth in accounting."

- ▲ Remember that **corporate managers play a role in accounting principle selection.** Managers may seek to enhance their own compensation or to reduce the possibility of violating loan agreements. They may also seek to reduce political costs.

CHAPTER SELF-TEST

Note: The notation (CO1) means that the question was drawn from chapter objective number one.

Matching

Please write the letters of the following terms in the spaces to the left of the definitions.

a. Change in accounting estimate
b. Change in accounting principle
c. Change in reporting entity
d. Relevance
e. Reliability
f. 10-K report
g. 10-Q report

_____ 1. (CO4) Must be filed on a quarterly basis with the SEC.

_____ 2. (CO6) Quality of accounting information which refers to an item's capacity to make a difference in a decision.

_____ 3. (CO1) Occurs when a firm changes the specific subsidiaries included in its consolidated financial statements.

_____ 4. (CO4) Must be filed on an annual basis with the SEC.

_____ 5. (CO1) Must be accounted for currently and prospectively.

_____ 6. (CO1) Occurs when a firm changes the method with which it accounts for a particular item.

_____ 7. (CO6) Quality of accounting information which refers to an item's integrity.

Completion

Please write in the word or words which will complete the sentence.

1. (CO1) The general rule for a change in accounting principle requires a _____________ _____________ adjustment.

2. (CO1) GAAP requires note disclosure of what net income would have been in current and prior years when there is a change in accounting principle, and these amounts are called _____________ _____________ amounts.

3. (CO1) A change in accounting principle is said to be accounted for _____________ when GAAP requires that prior years' financial statements be restated to reflect the change.

4. (CO2) An _____________ _____________ is a component of a firm that provides a product or service to unaffiliated customers.

5. (CO2) Firms are required to disclose if sales to a single customer exceed _____________ % of revenue.

6. (CO3) _____________ is the part of an annual report which contains an analysis of past performance and known trends.

7. (CO5) The _____________ _____________ _____________ states that publicly available information is fully reflected in share prices of stock.

8. (CO5) A corporate manager who _____________ the EMH probably will not try to affect share price by using accounting ploys to influence reported earnings.

9. (CO6) One of financial accounting's two roles is to serve as a basis for _____________.

10. (CO1) Changing the method of accounting for long-term construction contracts is a change in accounting _____________.

Multiple Choice

Please circle the correct answer.

1. (CO1) Which of the following statements is correct?
   a. The only way to account for a change in accounting principle is with a cumulative effect adjustment.
   b. The only way to account for a change in accounting principle is with a retroactive restatement of the financial statements.
   c. The only way to account for a change in accounting principle is currently and prospectively.
   d. Changes in accounting principle may be handled either with a cumulative effect adjustment or with a retroactive restatement of the financial statements.

2. (CO1) A company owns an asset which it has depreciated using sum-of-the-years'-digits depreciation for three years: The balance in the Accumulated Depreciation account is $6,500. In year four, the company decides to switch to straight-line depreciation. If the company had used straight-line for the previous three years, then the balance in the Accumulated Depreciation account would have been $3,000. What is the effect on the accounting equation in year four when the change in principle occurs?
   a. There is an increase in both Accumulated Depreciation and Cumulative Effect of Accounting Principle Change of $3,500.
   b. There is a decrease in Accumulated Depreciation and an increase in Cumulative Effect of Accounting Principle Change of $3,500.
   c. There is a decrease in Accumulated Depreciation and an increase in Cumulative Effect of Accounting Principle Change of $6,000.
   d. There is no effect. The company simply starts to use straight-line depreciation in year four.

3. (CO1) Which of the following changes in accounting principle is accounted for retroactively?
   a. A change from LIFO to another inventory method.
   b. A change in the method of accounting for long-term construction contracts.
   c. When required as part of the transition process for a new FASB standard.
   d. All of the above are accounted for retroactively.

4. (CO1) An asset has a cost of $10,000, a salvage value of $2,000, and an estimated useful life of 4 years. Straight-line depreciation is used. At the beginning of year 3, it is determined that the total life of the asset will be 6 years and that the salvage value will be $1,000. What will be the depreciation expense in year 3?
   a. $1,000.
   b. $1,250.
   c. $1,667.
   d. $2,000.

5. (CO1) A change in reporting entity is accounted for:
   a. retroactively.
   b. with a cumulative effect adjustment.
   c. currently and prospectively.
   d. in none of the above ways.

6. (CO2) Which of the following must a firm report for each major segment?
   a. Revenue.
   b. Operating profit or loss.
   c. Identifiable assets.
   d. A firm must report all of the above.

7. (CO3) Which of the following statements is <u>not</u> correct with respect to a firm's annual report?
   a. The report includes management discussion and analysis.
   b. The report includes forward-looking information.
   c. The report never includes forward-looking information.
   d. The report includes a listing of officers and directors.

8. (CO3) Which of the following statements is correct with respect to a firm's interim financial reports?
   a. Interim reports are exactly the same as the annual report: They just cover a shorter time period.
   b. Interim reports frequently require the use of additional estimates.
   c. Costs expensed for annual report purposes are always immediately expensed for interim reporting.
   d. None of the above statements is correct.

9. (CO6) The quality of accounting information which refers to an item's capacity to make a difference in a decision is:
   a. comparability.
   b. reliability.
   c. relevance.
   d. consistency.

10. (CO5) Which of the following statements about the efficient market hypothesis is true?
   a. All research evidence is consistent with the EMH.
   b. A corporate manager who accepts the EMH is likely to try to affect share price by using accounting ploys to influence reported earnings.
   c. An individual investor who accepts the EMH is likely to try to develop trading strategies based on publicly available information.
   d. The EMH states that publicly available information is fully reflected in share prices.

Demonstration Problems

1. A firm has an asset which cost $16,000 with a salvage value of $2,000 and an estimated useful life of 5 years. It has used double-declining balance depreciation for the first two years of the asset's life but has decided to switch to straight-line for the remaining years.

a. What is the depreciation expense for each of the first two years?

b. What would have been the effect, before taxes, on the accounting equation if straight-line depreciation had been used for the first two years?

c. How must the change in method be accounted for?

d. What will be the depreciation expense for the remaining three years of the asset's useful life?

2. A company owns an asset which cost $20,000 with a salvage value of $2,000 and an estimated useful life of 6 years. It uses straight-line depreciation. At the beginning of year 4, the company determines that the total life of the asset will be 8 years and that the salvage value will be $1,000.

a. What will be the depreciation expense in year 4?

b. How will the change be accounted for?

SOLUTIONS TO SELF-TEST

Matching

1. g
2. d
3. c
4. f
5. a
6. b
7. e

Completion

1. cumulative effect
2. pro forma
3. retroactively
4. industry segment
5. 10
6. management's discussion and analysis
7. efficient market hypothesis
8. accepts
9. engaging in contracts
10. principle

Multiple Choice

1. d
2. b
3. d
4. b
5. a
6. d
7. c
8. b
9. c
10. d

Demonstration Problems

1.

Remember that salvage value is ignored in the initial computation. The rate will be 40%, double the straight-line of 20% (100% ÷ 5 years).

a.

Year 1	$16,000 X 40% =	$ 6,400
Year 2	$ 9,600 X 40% =	$ 3,840
		$10,240

b. Years 1 and 2 $16,000 - $2,000 = $14,000 ÷ 5 years = $2,800
$2,800 + $2,800 = $5,600

Accumulated Depreciation would have been lower by $4,640 ($10,240 - $5,600), and Retained Earnings would have been higher by the same amount.

c. The change will be accounted for with a cumulative effect adjustment. Accumulated Depreciation will be reduced by $4,640, and Cumulative Effect of Accounting Principle Change will be increased by the same amount, thereby increasing Retained Earnings.

d. The remaining three years' depreciation will be the straight-line amount of $2,800 per year.

2.

a. Years 1 - 3 $20,000 - $2,000 = $18,000 ÷ 6 years = $3,000/yr.
Total Accumulated Depreciation is, therefore, $9,000.

The new book value is $11,000 ($20,000 - $9,000).
$11,000 - $1,000 = $10,000 ÷ 5 remaining years = $2,000/year

b. The change is a change in accounting estimate and will be accounted for currently and prospectively, meaning that the new depreciation expense will be used in the current year and in future years (until estimates change again, perhaps).

APPENDIX A

ACCOUNTING PROCEDURES

APPENDIX OVERVIEW

While the body of the textbook focuses on conceptual accounting issues and the uses of accounting information, the appendix shows the detailed procedures used by accountants to produce financial statements. You will see how numbers get into the accounting records and go through various procedures before they appear on the financial statements.

Review of Specific Appendix Objectives

1. Prepare and post journal entries.
2. Calculate account balances.

- ▲ Please remember that financial accounting is based upon the **accounting equation:** Assets = Liabilities + Owners' Equity. This is a mathematical equation which must balance. If assets total $300 and liabilities total $200, then owners' equity must be $100.

- ▲ An **account** is a mechanism which summarizes all the activity in one particular area, such as Cash or Accounts Payable. Regardless of the form of the account, the **left side of an account** is the debit side, while the **right side of an account** is the credit side. Do not associate "good" or "bad" with the words "debit" and "credit": They simply are directional, indicating left or right.

- ▲ It is critically **important to know what a debit and a credit do to a particular type of account.** Assets, withdrawals, and expenses act in similar fashion. Liabilities, owners' equity, and revenues act in similar fashion but **opposite to what assets, withdrawals, and expenses do.** Therefore, if a debit increases an asset, then it also increases withdrawals and expenses. If a debit increases this group, then a debit will do the opposite for liabilities, owners' equity, and revenues: A debit will decrease them. Remember that the debit side is the left side of an account, while the credit side is the right side. Therefore, if a debit increases assets, withdrawals, and expenses, then a credit will do the opposite: It will decrease them. If a debit decreases liabilities, owners' equity, and revenues, then a credit will do the opposite: It will increase them. Remember that assets are on the left side of the accounting equation and liabilities and owners' equity are on the right side. It seems logical that debits and credits will act in opposite fashion for the two sides of the equation.

▲ Most businesses have their own **chart of accounts**, which is a listing of the accounts used by the company and their account numbers. A common numbering protocol is that assets start with the number 1, liabilities with 2, owners' equity with 3, revenues with 4, and expenses with 5. **A collection of accounts is called the general ledger.** It can be produced manually or on a computer. To balance an account in the general ledger, the following is done: Debits are totaled, and credits are totaled. The two totals are subtracted one from the other, and the resulting difference is written on the side which had the larger total. Please note that **debits are added together and credits are added together but that a debit and a credit are subtracted one from the other.**

Cash	
1,000	
	500
	100
Bal 400	

▲ **Transactions of a firm are first entered into the general journal**, which provides a chronological listing of all transactions and events. Each journal entry consists of a date, the account(s) to be debited and credited, dollar amounts, and an explanation. If a firm collects $500 on an already billed account receivable on August 4, then the journal entry would be:

August 4	Cash	500	
	Accounts Receivable		500
	Collection on account.		

Debit account titles are listed first, and credits are listed second. Credits are always indented, which is a shorthand to indicate that that account has been credited in the journal entry. If accounts were listed under one another, then the eye would have to travel to the right side of the page to see which account had been credited. This would be extremely fatiguing. A **compound journal entry** has more than one account debited or credited (or both). The number of debit and credit account titles in an entry does not matter. What is important is that **the total dollar amount of debits and the total dollar amount of credits in the journal entry are equal.**

▲ If twenty-five journal entries were written in the general journal, all involving cash, then it would be time-consuming to determine the balance in the Cash account using just the journal. To facilitate keeping track of account balances, **the amounts in the general journal need to be transcribed, or posted, to the general ledger.**

▲ **Sales of inventory** contain both revenue and expense components. A **revenue transaction** exists because an asset has been obtained and goods have been provided to customers. An **expense transaction** exists because an asset has been consumed to generate the revenue. The resulting expense is called cost of goods sold. Therefore, **the sale of inventory involves two journal entries.** One of the entries records the retail sale by debiting Accounts Receivable and crediting Sales. The other entry removes the cost of the inventory from the Inventory account by debiting Cost of Goods Sold and crediting Inventory.

3. Prepare and post adjusting entries.

▲ **At the end of an accounting period,** before an income statement and a balance sheet can be prepared, **adjustments to certain accounts are almost always required.** A balance in an account may need to be adjusted because of the passage of time and the occurrence of events in that time period. In other cases, an amount may not have been recorded in an account at all, and the amount will have to be recorded before the financial statements are prepared so that all the information will be correct.

▲ **Commonly required adjusting journal entries** include those for the following:

Interest, which is a rental charge for the use of money. If the firm has a note or loan payable, then the adjusting entry will include a debit to Interest Expense and a credit to Interest Payable. If the firm has a note receivable, then the adjusting entry will include a debit to Interest Receivable and a credit to Interest Revenue.

Prepaid rent. If the firm has prepaid rent, then as time elapses, the asset is used up or consumed, and an expense is incurred. The adjusting entry will include a debit to Rent Expense and a credit to Prepaid Rent.

Depreciation, which shows that an asset such as equipment or a building is wearing out and being used up. The adjusting entry will include a debit to Depreciation Expense and a credit to the contra-asset account, Accumulated Depreciation.

Unearned revenue. If the firm has received cash in advance for services it must perform, then it will have earned revenue as time has elapsed because it has provided the service to the customer. The adjusting entry will include a debit to Unearned Revenue, a liability account, and a credit to a revenue account such as Service Revenue.

4. Prepare and post closing entries.

▲ **To close means to give a zero balance to an account.** Assume that an account has a $100 debit balance. If the accountant wishes to zero out that account, then he or she must write a journal entry crediting that account for $100. If an account has a $500 credit balance, then it must be debited for $500 in a journal entry in order to zero it out.

▲ **Revenues and expenses are closed.** These accounts are called temporary or nominal accounts. This is done so that retained earnings will show the effects of transactions in those accounts. In addition, since these accounts will have a zero balance at the end of one accounting period, they will only reflect the revenue and expense amounts for the next accounting period. Since expenses have debit balances, the closing entry will credit them and debit Retained Earnings. Since revenues have credit balances, the closing entry will debit them and credit Retained Earnings.

▲ **Payment of dividends also affects Retained Earnings.** When a dividend is paid, Retained Earnings is debited and Cash is credited.

5. Generate balance sheets and income statements from general ledger accounts.

▲ The **end result of the accounting process** is the preparation of financial statements. These are prepared by transfering the balances from the relevant general ledger accounts onto the appropriate financial statement.

▲ **A trial balance is a listing of all general ledger accounts with their appropriate debit or credit amounts.** It is constructed in order to check for the equality of debits and credits in the general ledger. They are usually prepared when an accountant has written and posted many journal entries so that he or she can check for errors.

- ▲ An **extended form of the trial balance** is the worksheet. It has two purposes: It contains a trial balance, and it provides a testing ground for adjusting and closing entries.

- ▲ The **purpose of a subsidiary ledger** is to provide detailed information regarding a particular general ledger account. For example, Accounts Payable will have the overall total amount owed to vendors and suppliers. The amount owed to each individual vendor or supplier will appear in one particular Accounts Payable subsidiary ledger account. When all posting is up to date, the total of the subsidiary ledgers should equal the balance in the Accounts Payable general ledger account. Accounts Receivable and the equipment accounts are others which often have subsidiary ledger detail.

- ▲ Accountants often use **special journals** to achieve efficiency and reduce possibility of errors in recording transactions. Types of special journals include the sales journal, purchases journal, cash receipts journal, and cash disbursements journal.

- ▲ **Regardless of whether an accounting system is manual or computerized, the accounting procedures are the same.** Computerized systems have several advantages over manual systems, however. They process transactions more quickly, they can achieve a greater degree of accuracy than do manual systems, and they permit a greater amount of information in the form of reports to be generated. A company which is considering computerizing its accounting operations must consider which **hardware** (physical components) to purchase and which **software** (instructions) to use.

APPENDIX SELF-TEST

Note: The notation (A1) means that the question was drawn from appendix objective number one.

Matching

Please write the letters of the following terms in the spaces to the left of the definitions.

a. Chart of accounts
b. Credit
c. Debit
d. General journal
e. General ledger
f. Posting

_____ 1. (A1,2) Right side of an account.

_____ 2. (A1,2) Process of transcribing numbers from the general journal to the general ledger.

_____ 3. (A1,2) Listing of account names and numbers used by a firm.

_____ 4. (A1,2) Place where numbers initially get into a firm's accounting system; chronological listing of transactions.

_____ 5. (A1,2) Collection of accounts.

_____ 6. (A1,2) Left side of an account.

Completion

Please write in the word or words which will complete the sentence.

1. (A3) The accrual of interest on a loan payable will involve a debit to Interest _________________________ and a credit to Interest _________________________.

2. (A4) In order to close its balance to Retained Earnings, a/an _________________________ will be credited in the closing journal entry.

3. (A4) Revenue and expense accounts are called _________________________ accounts.

4. (A5) The purpose of a _________________________ ledger is to provide detailed information regarding a particular general ledger account.

5. (A5) The purpose of __________________ __________________ is to help the accountant achieve efficiencies in journalizing transactions.

6. (A1,2) If an account has a debit total of $700 and a credit total of $300, then the overall balance in the account is a ___________________________ of ___________________________.

Multiple Choice

Please circle the correct answer.

1. (A1,2) Which of the following statements is correct?
   a. A debit increases a liability account.
   b. A credit increases an asset account.
   c. A debit increases an expense account.
   d. A credit decreases a liability account.

2. (A1,2) An account shows a debit of $500 and a debit of $1,000. It also shows a credit of $300 and a credit of $200. The balance in the account is:
   a. a debit of $1,000.
   b. a credit of $1,000.
   c. a debit of $1,500.
   d. a credit of $500.

3. (A5) An extended form of the trial balance is the:
   a. income statement.
   b. worksheet.
   c. balance sheet.
   d. statement of owners' equity.

4. (A1,2) If inventory is purchased on account, then the journal entry will:
   a. debit Accounts Payable and credit Inventory.
   b. debit Inventory and credit Cash.
   c. debit Inventory and credit Accounts Receivable.
   d. debit Inventory and credit Accounts Payable.

5. (A1,2) If $500 is received from customers for services to be performed in the future, then the journal entry will:
   a. debit Accounts Receivable and credit Unearned Revenue.
   b. debit Cash and credit Unearned Revenue.
   c. debit Cash and credit Service Revenue.
   d. debit Accounts Receivable and credit Unearned Revenue.

6. (A1,2) If inventory costing $1,000 is sold for $2,000, then the journal entry will include a:
   a. debit to Cost of Goods Sold for $2,000.
   b. credit to Cost of Goods Sold for $1,000.
   c. debit to Accounts Receivable for $2,000.
   d. credit to Accounts Receivable for $2,000.

7. (A3) If a firm uses $5,000 of prepaid rent, then the journal entry will include a:
   a. debit to Rent Expense for $5,000.
   b. debit to Cash for $5,000.
   c. credit to Cash for $5,000.
   d. debit to Prepaid Rent for $5,000.

8. (A3) The Service Revenue account has a balance of $3,000. When it is closed, the journal entry will include a:
   a. credit to Service Revenue.
   b. debit to Retained Earnings.
   c. debit to Cash.
   d. credit to Retained Earnings.

9. (A3) Which of the following is a temporary (or nominal) account?
   a. Accounts Receivable.
   b. Salaries Expense.
   c. Unearned Revenue.
   d. Retained Earnings.

10. (A5) An accountant proves the equality of debits and credits in the general ledger by preparing:
    a. a balance sheet.
    b. a income statement.
    c. a trial balance.
    d. None of the above is correct.

Demonstration Problem

The following are the transactions for the month of September 1998 for Trident Author's Service, owned and operated by Edna Boroski:

a. Edna started the business on September 1 with an investment of $20,000 cash.
b. On the 3rd, she paid rent of $2,000.
c. On the 4th, she received $500 from a client for services performed.
d. On the 7th, she purchased on account supplies costing $1,500.
e. On the 11th, Edna received cash in the amount of $120 for services performed.
f. On the 16th, she billed two clients for $750 each.
g. On the 18th, she received full payment from one client billed on the 16th.
h. On the 21st, she paid for the supplies purchased on the 7th.
i. On the 25th, she purchased on account equipment costing $4,500.
j. On the 27th, Edna returned $500 of the equipment purchased on the 25th.
k. On the 30th, Edna paid the utility bill of $300 and the telephone bill of $50.
l. On the 30th, she also withdrew $200 from the business for her personal use.

REQUIRED:

a. Please record the transactions in the general journal.

a. Continued

b. Please post the transactions to "T" accounts.

c. Please prepare a trial balance.

d. Please prepare an income statement, a statement of owner's equity, and a balance sheet.

d. Continued

SOLUTIONS TO SELF-TEST

Matching

1. b
2. f
3. a
4. d
5. e
6. c

Completion

1. Expense, Payable
2. credited
3. temporary (or nominal)
4. subsidiary
5. special journals
6. debit, $400

Multiple Choice

1. c
2. a
3. b
4. d
5. b
6. c
7. a
8. d
9. b
10. c

Demonstration Problem

a.

	Sept.			
a.	1	Cash	20,000	
		E. Boroski, Capital		20,000
		Investment of cash to start business.		
b.	3	Rent Expense	2,000	
		Cash		2,000
		Paid monthly rent.		
c.	4	Cash	500	
		Professional Fees		500
		Received cash for services performed.		
d.	7	Supplies	1,500	
		Accounts Payable		1,500
		Purchased supplies on account.		

e.	11	Cash	120	
		Professional Fees		120
		Received payment for services performed.		
f.	16	Accounts Receivable	1,500	
		Professional Fees		1,500
		Billed two clients for services performed.		
g.	18	Cash	750	
		Accounts Receivable		750
		Received payment on account from one client.		
h.	21	Accounts Payable	1,500	
		Cash		1,500
		Paid in full for supplies purchased on the 7th.		
i.	25	Equipment	4,500	
		Accounts Payable		4,500
		Purchased equipment on account.		
j.	27	Accounts Payable	500	
		Equipment		500
		Returned $500 of equipment purchased on the 25th.		
l.	30	Utilities Expense	300	
		Telephone Expense	50	
		Cash		350
		Paid monthly bills.		
m.	30	E. Boroski, Withdrawals	200	
		Cash		200
		Owner withdrew cash for personal use.		

b.

Cash

20,000	
	2,000
500	
120	
750	
	1,500
	350
	200
Bal 17,320	

Accounts Receivable

1,500	
	750
Bal 750	

Supplies

1,500	

Equipment

4,500	
	500
Bal 4,000	

Accounts Payable

	1,500
1,500	
	4,500
500	
	Bal 4,000

Edna Boroski, Capital

	20,000

Edna Boroski, Withdrawals

200	

Professional Fees

	500
	120
	1,500
	Bal 2,120

Rent Expense

2,000	

Utilities Expense

300	

Telephone Expense

50	

c.

Trident Author's Service
Trial Balance
September 30, 1998

Cash	$17,320	
Accounts Receivable	750	
Supplies	1,500	
Equipment	4,000	
Accounts Payable		$ 4,000
Edna Boroski, Capital		20,000
Edna Boroski, Withdrawals	200	
Professional Fees		2,120
Rent Expense	2,000	
Utilities Expense	300	
Telephone Expense	50	
	$26,120	$26,120

d.

Trident Author's Service
Income Statement
For the Month Ended September 30, 1998

Revenue:		
Professional Fees		$2,120
Expenses:		
Rent	$2,000	
Utilities	300	
Telephone	50	
Total Expenses		2,350
Net Loss		($ 230)

Trident Author's Service
Statement of Owner's Equity
For the Month Ended September 30, 1998

E. Boroski, Capital, September 1, 1998		$ 0
Add: Investment during the month		20,000
Subtotal		$20,000
Less: Net Loss	$230	
Withdrawals	200	
Net Decrease in Capital		430
E. Boroski, Capital, Sept. 30, 1998		$19,570

Trident Author's Service
Balance Sheet
September 30, 1998

Assets

Current Assets		
Cash	$17,320	
Accounts Receivable	750	
Supplies	1,500	
Total Current Assets		$19,570
Property, Plant, and Equipment		
Equipment		4,000
Total Assets		$23,570

Liabilities

Current Liabilities	
Accounts Payable	$ 4,000

Owner's Equity

Edna Boroski, Capital	19,570
Total Liabilities and Owner's Equity	$23,570